COMMAND AND CONTROL

Air Force Doctrine Document 6-0
1 June 2007

Incorporating Change 1, 28 July 2011

This document complements related discussion found in Joint Publication (JP) JP 1, *Doctrine for the Armed Forces of the United States*; JP 3-30, *Command and Control for Joint Air Operations*; and JP 6-0, *Joint Communications System*.

Cover Sheet for Air Force Doctrine Document (AFDD) 6-0, *Command and Control*

OPR: LeMay Center/DD

28 July 2011

AFDD numbering has changed to correspond with the joint doctrine publication numbering architecture (the AFDD titles remain unchanged until the doctrine is revised). Any AFDD citations within the documents will list the old AFDD numbers until the doctrine is revised. The changed numbers follow:

OLD	NEW	TITLE
AFDD 2-1	changed to AFDD 3-1	*Air Warfare*
AFDD 2-1.1	changed to AFDD 3-01	*Counterair Operations*
AFDD 2-1.2	changed to AFDD 3-70	*Strategic Attack*
AFDD 2-1.3	changed to AFDD 3-03	*Counterland Operations*
AFDD 2-1.4	changed to AFDD 3-04	*Countersea Operations*
AFDD 2-1.6	changed to AFDD 3-50	*Personnel Recovery Operations*
AFDD 2-1.7	changed to AFDD 3-52	*Airspace Control*
AFDD 2-1.8	changed to AFDD 3-40	*Counter-CBRN*
AFDD 2-1.9	changed to AFDD 3-60	*Targeting*
AFDD 2-10	changed to AFDD 3-27	*Homeland Operations*
AFDD 2-12	changed to AFDD 3-72	*Nuclear Operations*
AFDD 2-2	changed to AFDD 3-14	*Space Operations*
AFDD 2-2.1	changed to AFDD 3-14.1	*Counterspace Operations*
AFDD 2-3	changed to AFDD 3-24	*Irregular Warfare*
AFDD 2-3.1	changed to AFDD 3-22	*Foreign Internal Defense*
AFDD 2-4	changed to AFDD 4-0	*Combat Support*
AFDD 2-4.1	changed to AFDD 3-10	*Force Protection*
AFDD 2-4.2	changed to AFDD 4-02	*Health Services*
AFDD 2-4.4	changed to AFDD 4-11	*Bases, Infrastructure, and Facilities* [Rescinded]
AFDD 2-4.5	changed to AFDD 1-04	*Legal Support*
AFDD 2-5	changed to AFDD 3-13	*Information Operations*
AFDD 2-5.1	changed to AFDD 3-13.1	*Electronic Warfare*
AFDD 2-5.3	changed to AFDD 3-61	*Public Affairs Operations*
AFDD 2-6	changed to AFDD 3-17	*Air Mobility Operations*
AFDD 2-7	changed to AFDD 3-05	*Special Operations*
AFDD 2-8	changed to AFDD 6-0	*Command and Control*
AFDD 2-9	changed to AFDD 2-0	*ISR Operations*
AFDD 2-9.1	changed to AFDD 3-59	*Weather Operations*

BY ORDER OF THE
SECRETARY OF THE AIR FORCE

AIR FORCE DOCTRINE DOCUMENT 6-0
1 JUNE 2007
INCORPORATING CHANGE 1, 28 JULY 2011 |

SUMMARY OF CHANGES

This Interim change to Air Force Doctrine Document (AFDD) 2-8 changes the cover to AFDD 6-0 to reflect revised AFI 10-1301, Air Force Doctrine (9 August 2010). AFDD numbering has changed to correspond with the joint doctrine publication numbering architecture. AFI 10-1301 designates the title for this AFDD as *Command and Control Systems*. This interim change only changes the publication cover; therefore the content throughout the publication reflects the legacy title *Command and Control*. Once the content of this publication is fully revised, the cover will reflect the new title. A margin bar indicates newly revised material.

Supersedes: AFDD 2-8, 16 February 2001
OPR: LeMay Center/DD
Certified by: LeMay Center/DD (Col Todd C. Westhauser)
Pages: 120
Accessibility: Available on the e-publishing website at www.e-publishing.af.mil for
            downloading
Releasability: There are no releasability restrictions on this publication
Approved by: LeMay Center/CC, Maj Gen Thomas K. Andersen, USAF
            Commander, LeMay Center for Doctrine Development and Education

FOREWORD

The Air Force mission is global. Airmen are trained to employ air, space, and cyberspace forces anywhere, at any time, across the full range of military operations. In order to adequately support the Secretary of Defense and the geographic combatant commanders in executing operations, we must have a global command and control system. Military operations in the 21st century are highly complex and require close coordination to be effective. An effective command and control system allows efficient and effective coordination of all the means that Airmen can bring to bear on a conflict and speed the outcome in our favor.

"Command and control" is one of the key operational functions as described in Air Force Doctrine Document 1, *Air Force Basic Doctrine*. It is the key operational function that ties all the others together to achieve our military objectives. Our doctrine for command and control rests on the Air Force tenets of centralized control and decentralized execution. A commander of Air Force forces will be designated whenever Air Force forces are presented to a joint force commander. This designation provides unity of command. An Airman is normally designated as the joint force air and space component commander, resulting in clear lines of authority for both joint and Air Force component operations. We organize, train, and equip Airmen to execute the myriad tasks of command and control of air, space, and cyberspace forces through Air Force global and theater command and control systems.

Command and control of air and space power is an Air Force-provided asymmetric capability that no other Service or nation provides. We use a variety of means to leverage this capability. While we employ our command and control through various systems, our focus is on our most important asset, our people. All Airmen must be trained and educated to be command and control professionals. While we have a cadre of command and control operators, most Airmen will use the principles and tenets of command and control in employing forces at some point in their service to our nation. We must be prepared through effective training and education to perform these critical tasks.

Our doctrine is broadly stated to fit varying levels of contingencies and diverse geographical areas, while encompassing joint and multinational operations. Our doctrine will support effective employment of the various Air Force capabilities necessary to achieve an effects-based approach to operations. Airmen conduct operations and learn from those experiences every day. They are finding innovative ways to improve our command and control processes and technical capabilities. We must use these experiences to improve our doctrine to continue to support our national military objectives worldwide.

T. MICHAEL MOSELEY
General, USAF
Chief of Staff

TABLE OF CONTENTS

INTRODUCTION

PURPOSE

This Air Force Doctrine Document (AFDD) establishes doctrinal guidance for command and control operations to support national military objectives and commanders in employing air and space forces across the full range of military operations.

APPLICATION

This AFDD applies to the Total Force: all Air Force military and civilian personnel, including regular, Air Force Reserve, and Air National Guard units and members. Unless specifically stated otherwise, Air Force doctrine applies to the full range of military operations.

The doctrine in this document is authoritative, but not directive. Therefore, commanders need to consider the contents of this AFDD and the particular situation when accomplishing their missions. Airmen should read it, discuss it, and practice it.

SCOPE

This command and control doctrine is broad in nature and is adaptable to diverse global and theater-specific force deployment situations and differing levels of conflict. AFDD 2-8, *Command and Control,* is the keystone document addressing the spectrum of command and control functions that operate across the full range of military operations. It stresses the need for fixed and mobile, interoperable command and control centers, with efficient processes, state-of-the-art equipment, and properly trained Airmen to support US and multinational requirements worldwide.

COMAFFOR / JFACC / CFACC
A note on terminology

One of the cornerstones of Air Force doctrine is that "the US Air Force prefers - and in fact, plans and trains - to employ through a commander, Air Force forces (COMAFFOR) who is also dual-hatted as a joint force air and space component commander (JFACC)." (AFDD 1)

To simplify the use of nomenclature, Air Force doctrine documents will assume the COMAFFOR is dual-hatted as the JFACC unless specifically stated otherwise. The term "COMAFFOR" refers to the Air Force Service component commander while the term "JFACC" refers to a joint component-level operational commander.

While both joint and Air Force doctrine state that one individual will normally be dual-hatted as COMAFFOR and JFACC, the two responsibilities are different, and should be executed through different staffs.

Normally, the COMAFFOR function executes operational control/ administrative control of assigned and attached Air Force forces through a Service A-staff while the JFACC function executes tactical control of joint air and space component forces through an air and space operations center (AOC).

When multinational operations are involved, the JFACC becomes a combined force air and space component commander (CFACC). Likewise, the air and space operations center, though commonly referred to as an AOC, in joint or combined operations is correctly known as a JAOC or CAOC. Since nearly every operation the US conducts will involve international partners, this publication uses the terms CFACC and CAOC throughout to emphasize the doctrine's applicability to multi-national operations.

FOUNDATIONAL DOCTRINE STATEMENTS

Foundational doctrine statements are the basic principles and beliefs upon which AFDDs are built. Other information in the AFDD expands on or supports these statements.

✪ Effective command and control (C2) of forces is woven throughout each level of conflict and is accepted as a necessity for successful military operations. (Page 4)

✪ Centralized C2 of air and space forces under a single Airman is a fundamental principle of air and space doctrine. (Page 7)

✪ Unity of command is a principle of C2 operations. (Page 10)

✪ Centralized control and decentralized execution are tenets of C2 and provide commanders the ability to exploit the speed, flexibility, and versatility of global air and space power. (Page 12)

✪ Command may be delegated to another commander, but never to a staff. (Page 24)

✪ Air Force forces are presented to joint force commanders in a single, capabilities-based entity—the air and space expeditionary task force. (Page 33)

✪ A commander of Air Force forces is designated whenever Air Force forces are presented to a joint force commander. (Page 52)

✪ Planning is one process essential to effectively commanding and controlling military operations. (Page 70)

✪ Commanders must be provided with tools for decision-making through effective control, exploitation, and protection of information regardless of form or function. (Page 80)

✪ Specialized training and education of C2 professionals improves combat effectiveness; makes C2 capabilities universally understood, accepted, and exploitable by joint forces; and creates military and civilian C2 experts and leaders with a stronger foundation in force employment and capabilities. (Page 89)

CHAPTER ONE

FOUNDATIONS OF COMMAND AND CONTROL (C2)

The Operational Environment

Command and control are essential and integral parts of warfighting that require careful planning and execution to be effective. Early twentieth century air and space pioneers were quick to recognize that air warfare requires an intuitive and fast decision cycle. Commanders need to make timely decisions, based upon the best information available to them. Once decisions have been made, they need to be able to disseminate guidance and commander's intent to subordinate commanders and supporting commanders. This information enables collaboration (for supporting commanders), decision-making, and synchronization of operations. Commanders also need information to be fed back to them to enable the next decision.

Air and space capabilities can be most fully exploited when considered as an indivisible whole. Air Force operations and C2 are intimately related. With the advent of the airplane, a commander's area of focus grew a hundredfold larger. Today the United States conducts operations in an operational environment that is ever expanding.

The art of commanding Air Force forces lies in the ability to effectively integrate people, systems, and processes to enable sound decisions and produce the desired effects that support achievement of national objectives. Effective C2 capabilities support operations across the domains of air and space from the strategic to the tactical level of operations. Airmen should think in terms of controlling and exploiting the full air and space continuum on a regional and global scale to achieve desired effects. Air and space operations centers (AOCs) are becoming more capable of gathering and fusing the full range of information, from national to tactical, in real time, and rapidly converting that information to knowledge and understanding—to assure decision superiority over adversaries. This brings into focus the driving issues that affect Air Force C2. Effective C2 is essential to the Air Force in producing the right effects at the right place and time to support theater and global force commanders. The immense expanse of the global operational environment demands highly trained people, state-of-the-art technology, and efficient processes for successful C2. Modern conflicts demand fast and efficient C2 operations that are sufficiently flexible and adaptable to minimize the inevitable fog and friction of warfare.

To command effectively, commanders need a mechanism to exercise C2. Commanders give direction and guidance face to face at the unit level. In this construct, the C2 process is very simple. At higher levels the C2 process becomes more complex and commanders need a C2 system that ties together geographically separated units or those with diverse missions. The command mechanism at higher levels should consist primarily of C2 centers that are tailored to their unique requirements, based on their respective missions, geographic location, multinational situation, or makeup of the coalition. These C2 centers should be standardized to a certain extent, providing common technological and procedural requirements. They may be fixed, transportable, or mobile. They should provide commanders the capability to communicate up and down the chain of command, as well as laterally with commanders of other components or a coalition.

C2 is an Air Force function that affects Airmen at each level of command, in every theater, and across the range of military operations when air and space operations are conducted. Whether disseminating guidance to subordinate units, or receiving guidance from above, C2 enables successful operations. Throughout history, military forces sought ways to improve C2 operations. Runners were used to communicate between fielded forces. Semaphores and other visual signals were used between ships. The telegraph was used between fielded forces and their command elements. Each of these technological improvements in C2 granted an edge to the force adapting the technology for its use. These technological advances have usually been short-lived. Military forces of the United States have had and expect to continue to have a technological advantage over our adversaries, both in weapons capabilities and in the C2 systems that facilitate their employment. There is a continuing requirement to develop and enhance our fundamental concepts for effective C2, commensurate with our technical advantages. Effective preparation of C2 systems and the C2 professionals who employ them are both required to support military operations in today's highly volatile world situation. This preparation is a necessity to support tomorrow's fully integrated electronic battlefield.

C2 Defined

To frame the discussion of C2, the concept must be defined. Understanding C2 requires examining the definition found in Joint Publication (JP) 1-02, *Department of Defense (DOD) Dictionary of Military and Associated Terms*:

> The exercise of authority and direction by a properly designated commander over assigned and attached forces in the accomplishment of the mission. C2 functions are performed through an arrangement of personnel, equipment, communications, facilities, and procedures employed by a commander in planning, directing, coordinating, and controlling forces and operations in the accomplishment of the mission.

This definition acknowledges three central themes. The first theme, **personnel**, covers the human aspects of C2. In the context of this document, we refer to personnel as Airmen; the total force of regular Air Force, Air Force Reserve, Air National Guard of the US, and DOD civilians who serve the Air Force. The second, the **technology** element; covers the equipment, communications, and facilities needed to overcome the warfighting problems of integrating actions and effects across space and time. **Technology elements tend to dominate C2 doctrine**, because advanced technology characterizes American warfare. Technology can include equipment, facilities, hardware, software, infrastructure, materiel, systems, and a whole host of other elements. The third theme, labeled in this document as "**processes**," encompasses "procedures." This document extracts doctrinal concepts from generalized C2 processes. The details of C2 processes and associated procedures are found in tactics, techniques, and procedures documents and other instructional publications. Personnel, technology, and processes must all come together to efficiently execute C2 functions. Figure 1.1 portrays the Air Force C2 construct, which expands on the joint definition of C2. The construct reflects the processes, technology, and Airmen (personnel) mentioned in the joint definition of C2, and adds information as an element. These elements work together to enable effective decision-making by the organization's commander, who is at the center of the construct. The construct portrays C2 as the lens through which Air Force forces are transformed into air and space power, and it enables accomplishment of the mission.

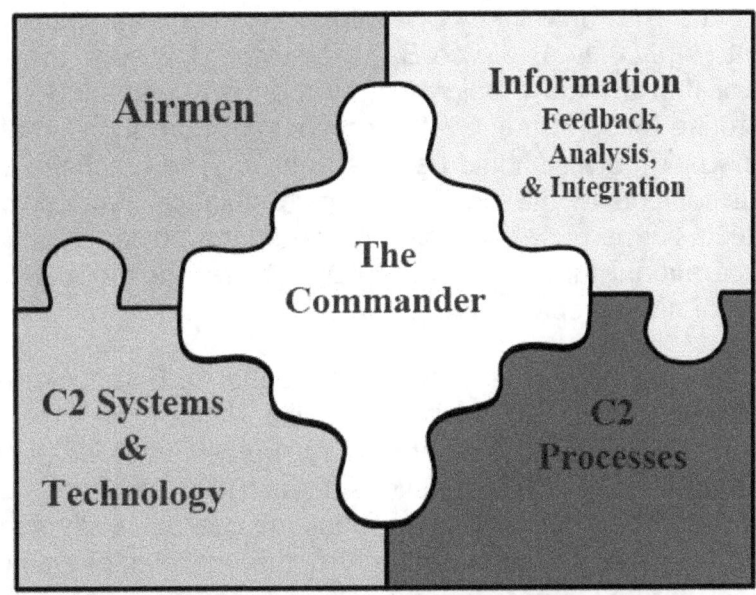

Figure 1.1. The Air Force C2 Construct.

C2 is not unique from other military functions. It enables mission accomplishment by collaborative planning and synchronizing forces and operations in time and purpose. Effective C2 enables a commander to use available forces at the right place and time to optimize the attributes of global vigilance, reach, and power, thereby allowing decision superiority over adversaries. Good horizontal and vertical information flow enables effective C2 throughout the chain of command. This information flow, and its timely fusion, enable optimum decision-making. This allows the centralized control and decentralized execution so essential to effective command of forces. A robust and redundant C2 system provides commanders the ability to effectively employ their forces despite the "fog and friction of war," while simultaneously minimizing the enemy's capability to interfere with the same.

Facilitating timely and informed decisions is at the heart of C2. Technological advances in the transfer and handling of information have created the information age. Advancements such as the global information grid (GIG) have accelerated the process of information sharing immensely. This capability foreshadows new opportunities for informed decision-making. It can, at the same time, threaten commanders with "information overload," challenging their ability to synthesize data and make timely decisions. Therefore, the identification of mission-essential information is paramount to successful information flow. Commanders and their staffs have a process for information flow, both within the headquarters or C2 center, or up and down the chain of command. This process should be formally documented in an information management plan (IMP). A portion of this information is provided by tools available to the commander, such as the commander's estimate of the situation, course of action (COA) selection, and detailed plans. By analyzing these and other products, commanders can determine the information they need to conduct operations and filter out the unnecessary.

C2 is one of the Air Force's key operational functions as described in Air Force Doctrine Document (AFDD) 1, *Air Force Basic Doctrine*. C2 as a construct fits in with the principles of war that are universally held by the joint community. The tenets of air and space power refine these further by adding context, from the Airman's perspective, about how air and space power should best be applied. The functions of air and space power take this discussion to the next level of granularity, by describing the actual operational constructs Airmen use to apply air and space power to achieve objectives. The Air Force's operational functions (see AFDD 1) are the broad, fundamental, and continuing activities of air and space power.

These functions are not necessarily unique to the Air Force. Some, including C2, predate air and space power as a separate military discipline. They have evolved steadily since air and space power's inception. Air Force forces employ air and space power globally through these basic functions to achieve strategic, operational, and tactical level objectives. These battle-proven functions can be conducted at any level of war and enable the Air Force to shape and control the operational environment. As one of these functions, **effective C2 of forces is woven throughout each level of conflict and is accepted as a necessity for successful military operations.**

C2, as one of the basic constructs Airmen use to employ air and space power, is one of the functions that cuts across all other functions in the Air Force. C2 cannot occur without the other functions. Likewise, if C2 of forces is not present other Air Force functions are somewhat difficult, if not impossible, to conduct.

C2 is a commonly accepted term in military operations, even though its meaning can be interpreted in different ways. To frame a discussion of C2, we must break down its components for definition and analysis. By defining the terms separately and analyzing them, we can re-form the construct of C2 with a clearer concept of what C2 really entails.

COMMAND DEFINED

The concept and the principles underlying command have been in existence since militaries were formed, thousands of years ago. The concept of command encompasses certain powers, duties, and unique responsibilities not normally given to leaders in the public or private sector. The art of command must be exercised with care and should be awarded only to those who have demonstrated potential to selflessly lead others. JP 1-02 defines command as:

> The authority that a commander in the Armed Forces lawfully exercises over subordinates by virtue of rank or assignment. Command includes the authority and responsibility for effectively using available resources and for planning the employment of, organizing, directing, coordinating, and controlling military forces for the accomplishment of assigned missions. It also includes responsibility for health, welfare, morale, and discipline of assigned personnel.

Today's full spectrum employment of air and space forces requires command responsibility to also include force protection.

Commanders are given authority and responsibility to accomplish the mission assigned. *Although commanders may delegate authority to accomplish the mission, they cannot delegate the responsibility for the attainment of mission objectives.* A Service component commander, such as the commander, Air Force forces (COMAFFOR), normally has operational and administrative responsibilities and should have the proper levels of authority to accomplish the mission. Commanders must be aware of the authorities they are given and their relationship under that authority with superior, subordinate, and lateral force commanders. Command relationships should be clearly defined to obviate confusion in executing operations. The command of air and space power requires intricate knowledge of the capabilities of the forces to be employed, and a keen understanding of the joint force commander's (JFC's) (in multinational forces a combined forces commander's) intent, and the authorities of other component commanders.

CONTROL DEFINED

Control is the process and system by which commanders plan and guide operations. Commanders should rely on delegation of authorities and commander's intent as methods to control forces. However, just as in the discussion of command, although commanders may delegate authority to accomplish the mission, they cannot delegate the responsibility for the attainment of mission objectives. JP 1-02 defines control as:

> Authority that may be less than full command exercised by a commander over part of the activities of subordinate or other organizations.

This is the process by which commanders *plan, guide, and conduct operations.* The control process occurs before and during the operation. Control involves dynamic balances between commanders directing operations and allowing subordinates freedom of action. These processes require strong leaders who conduct assessment and evaluation of follow-up actions. Often time and distance factors limit the direct control of subordinates. Commanders should rely on delegation of authorities and 'commander's intent' as methods to control forces. The commander's intent should specify the goals, priorities, acceptable risks, and limits of the operation. Commanders influence operations and ensure mission success through other means, such as memoranda of agreement (MOAs), memoranda of understanding (MOUs), and designation of an executive agent for specific functions. These and other types of agreements are usually negotiated before operations commence.

COMMAND AND CONTROL

A discussion of C2 will bring a variety of viewpoints and perspectives, depending upon an Airman's unique experiences, or his/her respective role in a military operation. To a JFC, a discussion of C2 might revolve around orders received directly from the Secretary of Defense (SecDef) to execute a major combat operation. A discussion of C2 with a joint terminal attack controller (JTAC) might entail guidance received to control an aircraft delivering ordnance on an enemy position. Both discussions concern C2 of forces within a theater. To the JFC, the discussion is on the strategic or operational level of war. The JFC will work through his/her staff and subordinate commanders to translate and execute the guidance given to employ theater forces. The JTAC will execute that guidance after it has been disseminated through the component and joint C2 apparatus and translate it into a tactical application. The results of that tactical application of firepower by the JTAC and the flight of aircraft that he controlled are exchanged throughout the C2 system. Those results will be combined with other data and assessed. If needed, the tactical engagement, or one similar to it, will be repeated to attain the JFC's objectives.

A discussion of C2 with a supporting commander (one involving global strike or global mobility forces) might entail receiving JFC intent, rules of engagement (ROE), and agreement as to when or if control of strategic global assets will be handed off to a theater commander for tactical employment. The discussions will also involve when the control of the global assets are returned to the supporting commander so they can be planned to support other global operations. Discussions should concern C2 of global forces operating into a theater and C2 of forces within a theater. To the JFC, in this case, the discussion is at the strategic and operational levels of war. The JFC will work through his/her staff, subordinate commanders, and supporting commanders to translate and execute the intent and guidance given to tactically employ strategic forces and the allocated theater forces.

Supporting commanders have unique requirements for C2 of forces. These forces may be tasked with global support, such as space or airlift forces. They require the ability to quickly establish or adapt C2 structures across the force and within the staff tailored to the mission, and to create the processes that will enable horizontal and vertical collaboration. They must have alternatives for organizing the components and defining command relations, depending upon conditions within the command and area of responsibility (AOR) to be supported, with associated guidance on when and how to apply them.

Although every Airman might have an unofficial definition of C2, there are formal definitions at the joint and component level. In general terms, C2 includes the process of planning, directing, coordinating, and controlling forces and operations. C2 involves the integrated processes, organizational structures, personnel, equipment, facilities, information, and communications designed to enable a commander to exercise authority and direction across the range of military operations.

The concept of a C2 system is purposefully broad in scope. A discussion of C2 as a function should be differentiated from the discussion of a C2 system. Often the term C2 is narrowly construed as the highly visible technology elements of a C2 operation. A C2 system encompasses both equipment items such as satellite communication systems or computer systems, as well as the capabilities that support C2 of military forces. Airmen should strive to become knowledgeable of all facets of the C2 process, including concepts, functions, and hardware and software requirements.

Command and Control of Air and Space Forces

Air and space forces conduct the C2 function to achieve strategic, operational, and tactical objectives. Air Force forces are employed in a joint force context by a JFC. C2 of those forces can be through a Service component commander or a functional component commander if more than one Service's air and space assets are involved. This officer, the combined/joint force air and space component commander (C/JFACC), should normally be the Service commander with the preponderance of air and space assets and the capability to plan, task, and control joint air and space operations. **Centralized C2 of air and space forces under a single Airman is a fundamental tenet of Air Force doctrine.**

Operation DESERT STORM

One of the most serious joint issues to arise in Operation DESERT SHIELD was the control of air power. Lieutenant General Horner, Commander of [US Air Forces, Central Command] USCENTAF, proposed that all aviation come under a single commander, and he requested that the JFACC control the air effort. Given the large number of US and allied aircraft, it was clear that some control was necessary. None of the components wanted to give up control of their aircraft, yet innovative solutions were worked out on the scene. For example, the Marine Corps did not want their unique air/ground task forces to be broken up. [US Marine forces, Central Command] USMARFORCENT worked out an agreement prior to execution of the air operation plan. USMARFORCENT would support its organic forces and provide an agreed-upon number of fixed-wing sorties to USCENTCOM for its use.

—Joint Military Operations Historical Collection, 1997

Concepts for the Control of Forces

There are other concepts and tools that can aid a commander in control of forces. These concepts facilitate communications between commanders and subordinates. If used effectively, they can provide information to subordinates even when traditional means of communications are nonexistent, because they have been rehearsed before a conflict begins. Some of these concepts are discussed below.

One of the commander's tools is employing information management. Control of information is a prerequisite to maintaining C2 of an operation. Identifying, requesting, receiving, tracking, and disseminating the needed information allow decision-makers to make informed and timely decisions. Commanders and staffs develop procedures that manage the available information to ensure it is used effectively.

Implicit communication can also be used. Commanders seek to minimize restrictive control measures and detailed instructions; therefore, they must find efficient and effective ways to create cooperation and compliance. Commanders and their subordinates at all levels do this by fostering implicit communication and understanding with everyone in the chain of command.

Two joint C2 concepts that nurture implicit communications are *commander's intent and mission-type orders.* By expressing intent and direction through mission-type orders, the commander attempts to provide clear objectives and goals to enable his/her subordinates to execute the mission.

Also available is the concept of decision superiority. AFDD 2-5, *Information Operations*, defines decision superiority as "a competitive advantage, enabled by an ongoing situational awareness that allows commanders and their forces to make better-informed decisions and implement them faster than their adversaries can react. Decision superiority is about improving our ability to observe, orient, decide, and act (the OODA loop) faster and more effectively than the adversary. Decision superiority is a relationship between adversary and friendly OODA loop processes." The commander can get inside the adversary's decision and execution cycle by making more timely and informed decisions. Doing so generates adversary confusion and disorder and slows opponents. The commander who can gather information and make decisions faster and better will generate a quicker tempo of operations and gain a decided military advantage. This can be an asymmetric capability for US forces.

Interoperable support systems are a requirement for effective control. Intelligence, surveillance, and reconnaissance (ISR), and command, control, communications, and computer support systems must be responsive in real time to provide the JFC (both in a functional or a geographic combatant commander's role) with accurate, timely, relevant, and adequate information. Interoperable systems, designed to be employed in a layered and redundant construct, result in a robust C2 capability to support the JFC. This robust integration of C2 and ISR assets facilitates timely guidance and efficient information flow.

Integration of C2 and ISR assets of Service or functional components and those of coalition members enhances the flow of information to commanders and among users. By integrating systems and leveraging their individual capabilities, planners can maximize available coverage of C2 and ISR assets for the commander. Synchronization of these assets allows their use at the time or in the situations that are most beneficial to the JFC to support a battle plan. Assets can be coordinated to achieve specific objectives or to provide redundant coverage or communications connectivity. Attacks are coordinated among Service or functional components to bring varied weapons and capabilities of the joint/combined force to bear on the opposing force at the time of the commander's choosing and when the most favorable conditions exist to execute operations.

Battle rhythm discipline as a concept also enhances control of forces. Effective operations in a theater requires the synchronization of strategic, operational, and tactical processes, to ensure mission planning, preparation, and execution are coordinated. This process is called battle rhythm or operational rhythm. It is essentially a schedule of important events which should be synchronized with the other Service or functional components and combined forces within a theater.

Battle rhythm is a deliberate daily cycle of command, staff, and unit activities intended to synchronize current and future operations. Activities at each echelon must incorporate higher headquarters guidance and commander's intent, and subordinate units' requirements for mission planning, preparation, and execution. If one element of the task force is not following the battle rhythm, it can produce problems in planning and executing operations with other elements of the task force. Every command headquarters has a rhythm regulated by the flow of information and the decision cycle. The keys to capturing and maintaining control over the battle rhythm are simplicity and sensitivity to the Service components' and superior commander's battle rhythms.

Efficient use of the staff facilitates effective control. The primary objective the staff seeks to attain for the commander, and for subordinate commanders, is understanding or situational awareness. This is a prerequisite for commanders to anticipate opportunities and challenges.

Trust among the commanders and staffs in a joint force expand the senior commander's options and enhances flexibility, agility, and the freedom to take the initiative when conditions warrant. Mutual trust results from honest efforts to learn about and understand the capabilities that each member brings to the joint force: demonstrated competence and planning and training together.

The JFC has a functional system and structure for disseminating guidance to his/her staff and to deployed forces. The functional components also play a role in this process through their functional operational centers that disseminate guidance to fielded forces. The operations center that disseminates the JFC's guidance for the Air Force component is the AOC.

Commanders need the ability to review and possibly alter mission objectives during the execution phase of operations in order to achieve the desired effects given a change in the situation. Commanders can use the effects-based approach to operations (EBAO), which are operations that are planned, executed, assessed and adapted to influence or change system behavior or capabilities in order to achieve desired outcomes. EBAO is sometimes colloquially but incorrectly referred to as "effects-based operations," or EBO. EBAO encompasses planning, execution, and assessment, all of which support the commander. The key insights associated with EBAO are: effective operations must be part of a coherent plan that logically supports and ties all objectives and the end state together; the plan to achieve the objectives must guide employment; and means of measuring success and gaining feedback must be planned for and evaluated throughout execution. For more on EBAO, see AFDD 2, *Operations and Organization*.

KEY CONSIDERATIONS OF C2

There are key considerations that guide C2 operations just as in other air and space operations. These key considerations are used by commanders to enable effective decision-making and to aid in the successful conduct of military operations. These considerations use principles and tenets that are woven throughout the C2 process. Unity of command ensures concentration of effort for every objective under one responsible commander. **Unity of command is a principle of C2 operations**, which, in turn, assures unity of effort and is supported by the tenets of *centralized control* and *decentralized execution*. Another enduring tenet of C2 operations is *informed decision-making*. Informed and timely decision-making is the essence of decision superiority. When the right information is flowing horizontally and vertically in a timely manner, the commander is able to fuse together the needed information to make the best possible decision—thus gaining and maintaining decision superiority to dominate the operational environment. The commander will never have all the information desired. Accepting and taking reasonable risks to achieve mission success is the norm in warfare—efficient and effective C2 minimizes that risk.

Unity of Command

Unity of command is one of the principles of war. According to AFDD 1, *Air Force Basic Doctrine,* "Unity of command ensures the concentration of effort for every objective under one responsible commander. This principle emphasizes that all efforts should be directed and coordinated toward a common objective."

Nothing is more important than unity of command.

—Napoleon

Unity of command is not intended to promote centralized control without delegation of execution authority to subordinate commanders. Some commanders may fulfill their responsibilities by personally directing units to engage in missions or tasks. However, as the breadth of command expands to include the full spectrum of operations, commanders are normally precluded from doing so. Thus, C2 operations normally include the assignment of responsibilities and the delegation of authorities between superior and subordinate commanders. A reluctance to delegate decisions to subordinate commanders slows down C2 operations and takes away the subordinates' initiative. Senior commanders should provide the desired end-state, desired effects, ROE, and required feedback on the progress of the operation and not actually direct tactical operations.

As an example, some functions, such as counterair operations, must decentralize authority when the situation dictates. The area air defense commander (AADC) must decentralize engagement authority to sector air defense commanders if the integrated air defense system is overwhelmed by the sheer number of hostile tracks, or loss of communications with the air defense sectors occurs. In this case, the AADC cannot direct which targets should be engaged, and must rely on subordinate commanders to do so. Once effective communications are regained, or the tactical situation allows, the AADC can reassume engagement authority. Engagement authority is always spelled out in the ROE for an operation, as well as in governing documents such as the air defense plan. Responsibilities of commanders at each level must be clearly understood before decentralization of authority occurs.

Unity of command ensures concentration of effort for every objective under one responsible commander. This principle emphasizes that all efforts should be directed and coordinated toward a common objective. Air and space power's operational-level perspective calls for unity of command to gain the most effective and efficient application. Coordination may be achieved by cooperation; it is, however, best achieved by vesting a single commander with the authority to direct all force employment in pursuit of a common objective. The essence of successful operations is a coordinated and cooperative effort toward a commonly understood objective. In many operations, the wide-ranging interagency and non-governmental organization operations involved may dilute unity of command; nevertheless, a unity of effort must be preserved to ensure common focus and mutually supporting actions.

11

Unity of command is vital in employing forces. Air and space power is the product of multiple capabilities, and centralized C2 is essential to effectively fuse these capabilities. Airmen best understand the entire range of air and space power. An Airman may be designated as the supported commander for an operation or as the supporting commander. Whether in the role of supported or supporting commander, Air Forces are presented as a separate force to the JFC, under a single Airman, a COMAFFOR, to preserve unity of command. Air Force forces are not broken apart piecemeal under the component commanders being supported. Breaking Air Force forces apart dilutes their effectiveness. The ability of air and space power to range on a theater and global scale imposes responsibilities that can be discharged only through the integrating function of centralized control under an Airman. That is the essence of unity of command and air and space power.

There are exceptions to the tenets governing delegation of authorities to subordinate commanders. Some capabilities, such as nuclear forces, national missile defense systems and national-level ISR assets require centralized control. For example, JP 0-2, *Unified Action Armed Forces (UNAAF)*, states, "National policy requires centralized execution authority of nuclear weapons. The President is the sole authority for release of US nuclear weapons. The President's decision to authorize release of these weapons is based on recommendations of the SecDef, the Chairman of the Joint Chiefs of Staff (CJCS), geographic combatant commanders, and allies. The President will monitor all aspects of the authorization and employment of nuclear weapons." Delegation of authority for execution is not appropriate in employing these assets.

Centralized Control and Decentralized Execution

Centralized control and decentralized execution are key tenets of C2; they provide commanders the ability to exploit the speed, flexibility, and versatility of global air and space power. Centralized control is defined in JP 1-02 as, "In joint air operations, placing within one commander the responsibility and authority for planning, directing, and coordinating a military operation or group/category of operations." Air and space power's unique speed, range, and ability to maneuver in three dimensions depends on centralized control by an Airman to achieve effects when and where desired.

Centralized control and decentralized execution are critical to the effective employment of air and space power. Indeed, they are the fundamental organizing principles Airmen use for effective C2, having been proven over decades of experience as the most effective and efficient means of employing air and space power. Because of air and space power's unique potential to directly affect the strategic and operational levels of war, it must be controlled by a single Airman at the air component commander level. This Airman must maintain the broad strategic perspective necessary to balance and prioritize the use of the air and space resources that have been allocated to the theater. A single commander, focused on the broader aspects of an operation, can best mediate the competing demands for tactical support against the strategic and operational requirements of the conflict.

JP 0-2 embodies the Air Force's commitment to the tenet of centralized control of air and space power in its description of the fundamental concept of a functional component commander. The UNAAF outlines the requirement to place the responsibility for air operations under a single commander. AFDD 2, *Operations and Organization,* describes the joint air and space operations center (JAOC) where centralized planning, directing, controlling, coordinating, and assessing take place. A balance exists between too much and too little centralized control. Overcontrolling air and space power robs it of flexibility, taking away initiative from operators. Undercontrolling air and space power fails to capitalize on joint force integration and orchestration, thus reducing its effectiveness.

Centralized control of air and space forces levies a major requirement on Air Force C2 operations. This requirement is to establish and maintain two-way information flow among commanders, operators, and combat support elements that must be effectively integrated to achieve the desired combat effects. Using timely and available information, commanders make and communicate decisions. A good example is the air tasking order (ATO); it embodies command decisions that must be communicated to the operators. It enables the CFACC to control theater-wide air and space forces in support of the JFC's objectives. The ATO allows the JFC to integrate air and space operations across the theater, to bring forces to bear at the time and location of his/her choosing. It also allows air and space forces to be fully integrated to support the JFC's intent. The ATO is centrally planned and developed at the operational level, but its execution is decentralized to subordinate C2 nodes and tactical level units.

Senior commanders making operational decisions, combined with subordinates free to exercise initiative in executing those decisions, make up the heart of C2—centralized control and decentralized execution. There may be times when the political leadership becomes directly involved in the execution of military operations. This high-level political involvement tends to drive a higher level of centralized command. Decentralized execution in these instances may vary with the latitude granted by the senior national leadership. Coalition unity and collateral damage are two common concerns that may challenge the optimal balance in centralized control and decentralized execution.

Centralized control and decentralized execution of air and space power provide theater-wide focus while allowing operational flexibility to meet theater objectives. They assure concentration of effort while maintaining economy of force. They exploit air and space power's versatility and flexibility to ensure that air and space forces remain responsive, survivable, and sustainable.

**Case Study:
Failure to Decentralize and the Role of the Staff,
Major General George C. Kenney in the South Pacific, 1942**

On 4 August 1942, the day Kenney officially took command, he received orders for upcoming air operations. Rather than broad mission guidance, [Maj. Gen. Richard K.] Sutherland [Gen. MacArthur's Chief of Staff] sent detailed instructions, directing takeoff times, weapons, and even tactics. Kenney was furious. He immediately marched into Sutherland's office, arguing, in typical Kenney fashion, that he was the "most competent airman in the Pacific" and that he had the responsibility to decide how the air units should operate—not Sutherland. Kenney shot down Sutherland's rebuttal by suggesting that they "go into the next room, see General MacArthur, and get this thing straight. I want to find out who is supposed to run this Air Force." According to Kenney, Sutherland backed down, rescinded the orders, and then apologized, claiming that he had been forced to write the detailed instructions prior to Kenney's arrival.

Although this was not the final disagreement between the two, it was the last time Sutherland directly interfered with Kenney's combat operations. Perhaps the showdown vindicated [Lt Gen] Brett's [Kenney's predecessor's] analysis of Sutherland as a bully who backed down when someone stood up to him. More likely, both Sutherland and Kenney knew that the chief of staff should not have issued detailed orders to the air component commander and realized that MacArthur would back Kenney in this situation.

—Col Thomas E. Griffith,
*Command Relations at the Operational Level of War: Kenney,
MacArthur, and Arnold*

This example from World War II illustrates a violation of two tenets of command and control. The first was the principle of unity of command. Airpower was not unified under one commander if both the Chief of Staff and the air forces commander were issuing guidance on how it should be employed. The second tenet violated was the one that ensures unity of command *in commanders*, not staffs. *The staff is an extension of the commander*. Its sole function is command support, and its only authority is that which is delegated to it by the commander. *The "staff" cannot issue orders to subordinate elements*. The staff assists the commander.

The tenets of centralized control and decentralized execution also apply to global strategic forces, such as global strike or air mobility forces. Supporting and supported commanders must also consider the planning, direction, prioritization, synchronization, integration, and deconfliction of global forces supporting and integrating with theater operations. In this case, control of strategic forces may remain with the supporting commander until it is appropriate to transition control to the JFC for centralized control and tactical employment. Commanders need to consider and agree on who is best suited to control, plan, direct, and synchronize strategic, operational, and tactical operations. When global strategic forces are called on to support theater objectives, the CFACC and the combined air operations center (CAOC) should coordinate through their theater JFC with the supporting commanders and their AOCs to discuss control and execution of strategic missions as they are integrated with theater forces.

Centralized control of air and space power is the planning, direction, prioritization, synchronization, integration, and deconfliction of air and space capabilities to achieve the objectives of the JFC. It can be provided for any contingency across the range of military operations. Centralized control maximizes the flexibility and effectiveness of air and space power; however, it must not become a recipe for micromanagement, stifling the initiative subordinates need to deal with combat's inevitable uncertainties.

Decentralized execution is defined in JP 1-02 as, "Delegation of execution authority to subordinate commanders." Decentralized execution of air and space power is the delegation of execution authority to responsible and capable lower level commanders to achieve effective span of control and to foster disciplined initiative, situational responsiveness, and tactical flexibility. In other words, decentralized execution means that tactical commanders, whether in a theater or sector C2 center, in the cockpit, or in the field, retain the authority to make their own tactical decisions. It allows subordinates to exploit opportunities in rapidly changing, fluid situations. The benefits inherent in decentralized execution, however, are maximized only when a commander clearly communicates his/her intent to subordinates.

A key element in the concept of decentralized execution is the principle of delegation of execution authority. Even commanders at the lowest levels of responsibility cannot execute or directly oversee every task that is performed within their units or organizations. This situation is made much more complex for a theater or Service component commander. By delegating authority for certain key tasks, commanders can ensure their subordinates can execute decisions for them, while following their guidance disseminated via commander's intent.

Decentralized execution does not imply that subordinate commanders or those holding certain duty positions have free reign in accomplishing their directed tasks. In some cases free rein may be given. Usually commanders are given authority to act in certain situations and circumstances, within parameters established by the JFC or the Service component commander, such as commander's intent and ROE.

For example, the CFACC's responsibilities are assigned by the JFC, which will normally include delegation of authority to execute air and space operations. The CFACC's responsibilities will normally include developing a joint air and space operations plan (JAOP), assigning missions, tasking forces, and ensuring unity of effort in accomplishing the overall theater mission. The CFACC also delegates authority to enable mission accomplishment in a rapidly changing operational environment. In his/her role as AADC, the CFACC may delegate execution authority to engage hostile aircraft and missiles to regional or sector air defense commanders, or to elements of the theater air control system (TACS), when the situation requires it. This engagement authority is tightly prescribed to defensive counterair (DCA) operations, and is spelled out in the air defense plan and the theater ROE. The engagement authority given to regional air defense commanders enables them to influence DCA operations, but it does not necessarily allow them to influence other air operations.

> *Modern communications technology provides a temptation towards increasingly centralized execution of air and space power. Although several recent operations have employed some degrees of centralized execution, such command arrangements will not stand up in a fully stressed, dynamic combat environment, and as such should not become the norm for all air operations... A high level of centralized execution results in a rigid campaign unresponsive to local conditions and lacking in tactical flexibility. For this reason, execution should be decentralized within a C2 architecture... Nevertheless, in some situations, there may be valid reasons for execution of specific operations at higher levels, most notably when the JFC (or perhaps even higher authorities) may wish to control strategic effects, even at the sacrifice of tactical efficiency. These instances should be the exception, rather than the norm.*
>
> **—AFDD 1, *Air Force Basic Doctrine***

Continuing with the example, the authority to execute surface attack operations may be delegated from the CFACC to subordinate commanders or individuals qualified for certain duty positions, such as a senior offensive duty officer (SODO) in the AOC or an air liaison officer (ALO) in the tactical air control party (TACP). This delegated authority is used by the SODO in the AOC for planning surface attack operations. It is used by the ALO in the TACP for mission execution. The ALO has prescribed delegated authority from the CFACC to divert the supported ground commander's allocated surface attack missions to a higher priority tasking if the need arises.

Guidance for planning and conducting air and space operations is reflected in the commander's intent. Those granted delegated authority must understand the commander's intent, which is disseminated through the campaign plan and other plans and annexes that provide specific guidance for specialized functions. Unity of effort over complex operations is made possible through decentralized execution of centralized, overarching plans. Roles and responsibilities must be clearly spelled out and understood. Communication between commanders and those who are granted delegated authority is essential throughout all phases of the military operation.

ROE for the operation and host nation sensitivities must be considered. Each situation will vary due to the personalities of the commanders involved. The political and diplomatic situation will influence military operations. Guidance given to a JFC at the beginning of a conflict may change during the conflict. General MacArthur received a set of military objectives from the national leadership at the beginning of the Korean conflict. He was issued a set of objectives that were quite different after the Chinese crossed the Yalu River and attacked United Nations forces. The campaign plan was revised to accommodate the realities of the political and diplomatic situation at that time.

Centralized control and decentralized execution of air and space forces requires a two-way information flow between commanders. Subordinate commanders do not always have the situational awareness for theater and multinational concerns, as well as the intelligence information that senior commanders may have. The subordinate commanders may feel so restricted that they cannot exercise what they feel is their full range of military options to accomplish a task. Subordinate commanders must develop a sense of how far they can go while executing decentralized control. Authorities must be spelled out before operations commence.

Advances in information management and communications greatly enhance the situational awareness of tactical commanders, combatant commanders, and even the senior national leadership. These advances enhance the flow of shared knowledge, and more freely enable the communication of intent, ROE, desired effects, collaborative planning, and synchronized operations across the globe among commanders. These technological advances increase the potential for superiors, once focused solely on strategic and operational decision-making, to assert themselves at the tactical level. While this is their prerogative, it is done so with risk. Decentralized execution remains a basic C2 tenet of joint operations. The level of control used will depend on the nature of the operation or task, the risk or priority of its success, and the associated comfort level of the commander.

Informed Decision-Making

The C2 process should support informed and timely decisions at all levels of command. The process should be adapted to the circumstances presented by the mission and operational environment. The process should not be used blindly in a checklist fashion. A key attribute of informed decision-making is using available, processed, and sorted information to choose among competing COAs. Time-sensitive targeting decisions and sensor-to-shooter reactions are prime examples of competing COAs that must be reconciled by the air and space commander. Commanders preserve the flexibility of Air Force capabilities by making informed and timely decisions. Deferring decisions by moving them up or down the chain of command sacrifices the initiative and limits the flexibility of alternatives.

Commanders must have actionable information that has been sorted and processed. Today's information systems can process huge amounts of data and forward that data in near-real time. During a contingency, a commander usually cannot sort through a vast amount of data. There is simply too much data available and not enough time. The commander's staff must organize, filter, analyze, and sort through the data to forward what the commander actually needs to enable a decision. Commander and staff "information overload" could lead to missing a truly important piece of information while sorting through a mountain of data. An effective IMP is essential to mitigate the risk of information overload by defining who needs what information and how it will be presented.

Commanders are aided in the decision-making process by the concept of information superiority. Information superiority is an integral part of full spectrum decision superiority. AFDD 2-5, *Information Operations*, defines information superiority as "the ability to collect, control, exploit, and defend information without effective opposition." It includes both the ability to employ actionable intelligence/information to our advantage and to the disadvantage of our adversaries, as well as the freedom of action in the information environment.

Improvements in technology have aided in the efficient transmission of information. Technological improvements have eased, but not eliminated, the need for trained people to make assessments on the value of information. Airmen must continue to broker information for it to be useful to a commander. These trained professionals use formalized procedures in brokering the information. They are constantly seeking to improve their procedures for sifting information to provide the best possible situational awareness to the commander.

Centralized control of airpower was the only feasible means by which each of the ground forces [U.S., Republic of Vietnam, Korean, Australian corps] could get air support when it needed it. By early 1967, there were hundreds of thousands of troops in country. The 7th Air Force was well established by this time to support the U.S., ARVN, Korean, and Australian ground forces in all of the four corps areas. If the air had been divided-up among these various forces, COMUSMACV would have been unable to concentrate the airpower of 7th AF where he wanted and needed it. With the control centralized, he was able to move around anywhere within his area of responsibility concentrating firepower as needed.

—General William W. Momyer, USAF (Retired),
Airpower in Three Wars (WWII, Korea, Vietnam)

The GIG is a "system of systems" that enables faster decision-making. It is a combination of information systems constantly being improved and upgraded. The GIG will aid operators at all levels by making information more readily available and more easily shared among users. According to JP 1-02:

> The GIG is the globally interconnected, end-to-end set of information capabilities, associated processes and personnel for collecting, processing, storing, disseminating, and managing information on demand to warfighters, policy makers, and support personnel. The GIG includes all owned and leased communications and computing systems and services, software (including applications), data, security services, and other

associated services necessary to achieve information superiority. The GIG supports all DOD, national security, and related intelligence community missions and functions (strategic, operational, tactical, and business), across the full range of military operations. The GIG provides capabilities from all operating locations (bases, posts, camps, stations, facilities, mobile platforms, and deployed sites). The GIG provides interfaces to coalition, allied, and non-DOD users and systems.

A portion of the GIG, the defense information systems network (DISN) is an integrated network, centrally managed and configured, to provide telecommunications services for all DOD activities. The CJCS exercises operational oversight over the DISN through the National Military Command Center (NMCC) and the Defense Information Systems Agency (DISA) network operations and security center hierarchy. The overall C2 of the GIG is accomplished through a comprehensive system that distributes management and technical control functions to DOD components responsible for equipping the GIG, while integrating combatant commander operational oversight. United States Strategic Command (USSTRATCOM) has overall responsibility for GIG operations and defense in coordination with the CJCS and combatant commands.

Overall C2 of the Air Force portion of the GIG is provided by the concept of Air Force network operations, or AFNETOPS. The Eighth Air Force commander (8 AF/CC) is the COMAFFOR for Air Force forces conducting AFNETOPS in support of Joint Task Force-Global Network Operations (JTF-GNO). In the role of AFNETOPS commander (AFNETOPS/CC), 8 AF/CC is responsible for the day-to-day operations of the Air Force portion of the GIG. Currently, this is the Air Force's most visible manifestation of a distinctly separate cyberspace organization. AFNETOPS ensures reliable, redundant, and robust Air Force systems and networks are available to support commanders to establish and maintain the vertical and horizontal information flow essential to promote information and decision superiority. Disciplined operations aid in ensuring the availability of the global infrastructure vital to connecting these information resources.

The AFNETOPS/CC has the overall responsibility for ensuring the effective operation and the defense of the Air Force-provisioned portion of the GIG, throughout all levels of military operations. AFNETOPS C2 is accomplished through a structured framework to monitor, assess, plan, decide, and execute operations across fixed, mobile, terrestrial, airborne, and space facilities, assets, and equipment. It is conducted by trained personnel providing near real-time situational awareness, assessments, and courses of action for end-to-end control, operation, and defense of the network.

Information Integration

Integration of information among users is essential to effective C2. There is two-way information flow between commanders and operators, often depicted as a vertical or "up-and-down" flow. Commanders rely on vertical information flow to produce a common tactical picture of the battle. Senior commanders, like the JFC, may subsequently use several common tactical pictures to produce a tailorable, common operational picture (COP) of the tactical, operational, or strategic environment. Vertical information flow is fundamental to centralized control and important for direction and feedback. Without this flow, commanders cannot give meaningful feedback when controlling operations.

Another type of information flow is horizontal or "peer-to-peer" communication, which normally occurs between operators and other like elements. Horizontal information flow is essential for common situational awareness. Both vertical and horizontal information flow exchange data that, when fused in a timely manner, becomes integrated information to provide the framework for the commander to make the best possible decision enabling decision superiority. Decision superiority is a competitive advantage.

The dynamic fusion of vertical and horizontal information allows timely assessments and decisions by the air and space commander—centralized control. At the strategic, operational, and tactical levels, proper information fusion allows better situational awareness enabling decentralized execution. Figure 1.2 depicts the interrelationship of vertical and horizontal information flow for both theater and global operations. It represents a notional informational flow among C2 centers. It is not a wiring diagram showing command relationships.

Decentralized execution by air and space forces levies another major requirement on Air Force C2 operations. This requirement is to ensure the two-way horizontal information flow that reduces the uncertainty of war by enabling information to flow freely among operators. Horizontal flow of information enhances operator initiative. As the operational environment changes, operators are free to act within the guidelines of the commander's intent and rules of engagement. The balance between vertical and horizontal information flows should be described in the C2 section of the operation plan (OPLAN). Both the technology required and the procedures used to affect these vertical and horizontal information flows must be spelled out prior to a conflict, in the OPLAN or its C2 annex. Maintaining this balance of information flow across the full spectrum of air and space employment is a job for all Airmen.

Work still needs to be done to integrate horizontal and vertical information flows. When the vertical flow dominates, subordinate commanders and operators may suffer as the initiative is passed to senior commanders. When the horizontal flow dominates, commanders may suffer because they do not have the information necessary to exercise focused control of present operations and to plan future operations.

C2 processes are the structured basis of informed decision-making. Technology either automates or accelerates these processes via advances in information technology like digital electronic communications, computers, and expert systems. There is no substitute for trained personnel using intuition and common sense in making the final decision, however. Airmen, schooled in the art of war, need good information as well as an efficient and effective process to make the best-informed decisions.

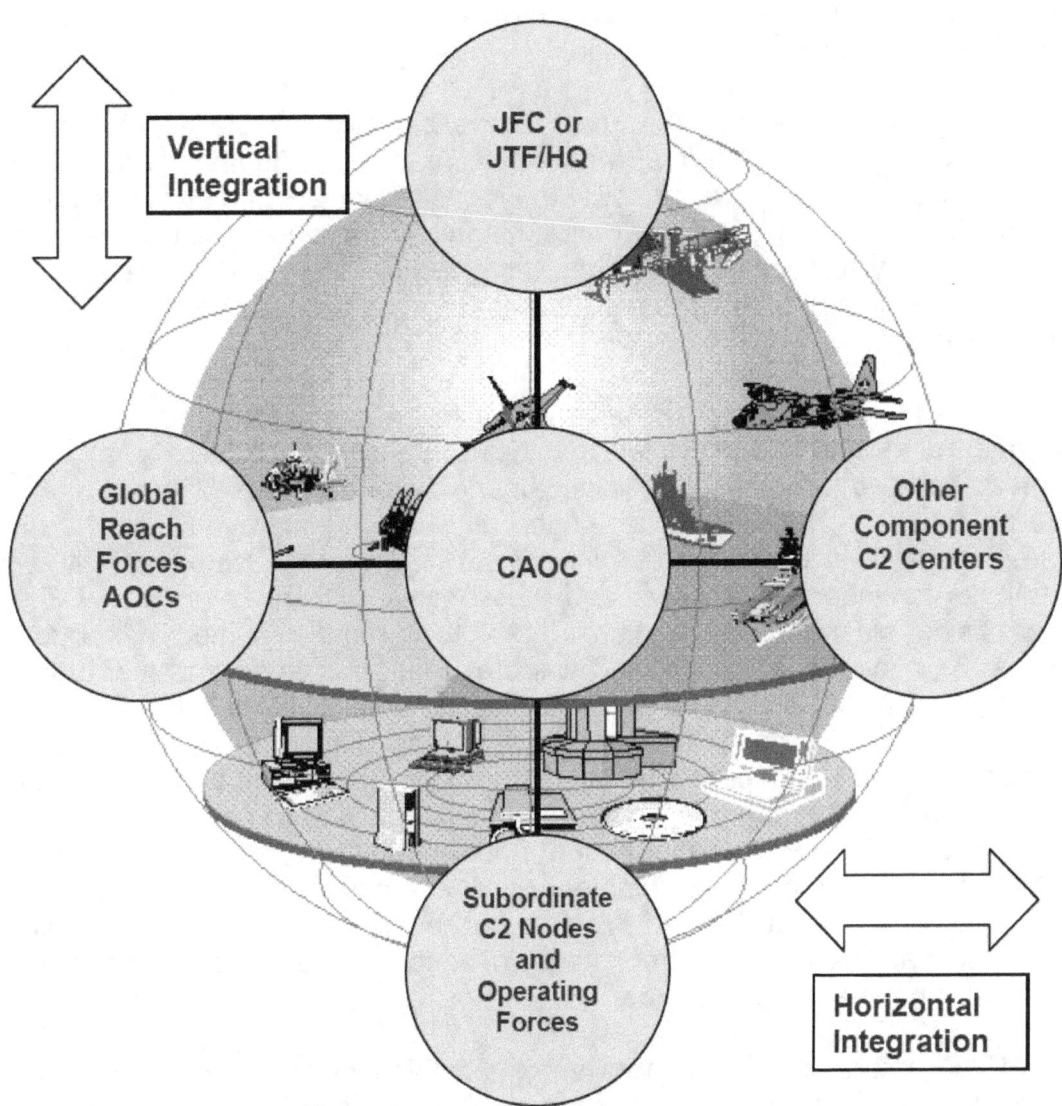

Figure 1.2. Information Integration.

Network-Centric Warfare

Improvements in technology and the flow of information have resulted in additional concepts affecting military operations such as network-centric warfare (NCW). NCW networks enable sensors, decision makers, and combat forces to achieve shared awareness, increased speed of command, a higher tempo of operations, greater lethality, increased survivability, and a degree of operational synergy. In essence, it translates information advantage into combat power. It effectively links friendly forces within the operational environment and provides a much improved shared awareness of the situation. Net-centricity enables the collection of data and information for fusion flowing from surface forces; multi-mission air and space platforms; and computer networks, together with analytically derived knowledge. It enables more rapid and effective decision-making at all levels of military operations. NCW allows for increased speed of execution. The NCW construct is underpinned by information technology systems, but it requires trained and knowledgeable Airmen to enable its inherent advantages to support military operations.

During the 1990s, the Air Force made significant progress in improving its information superiority capabilities. It greatly increased the number of quality sensors, multisensor platforms, and the capability to process, analyze, and distribute data quickly over vast distances. This led to an order of magnitude increase in situational awareness and the capability to conduct operations more flexibly and rapidly. The Air Force has actively pursued interoperability for its C2 and ISR systems, leading the DOD's network-centric initiatives.

The Air Force views NCW as the natural progression of technology and employment that aids in the efficient transfer of data to warfighters at all levels. The attributes of shared awareness, decision superiority, and increased speed of execution; touted as central to NCW, have developed and steadily improved over the history of warfare. The earliest commanders of fielded forces communicated directly with their subordinate commanders or they used messengers to convey orders. C2 systems evolved using means such as signal fires, flags, and mounted riders to convey guidance. This level of C2 supported warfare in ancient times and the Middle Ages, consisting primarily of conflict between forces on a relatively localized battlefield. As warfare expanded to conflicts on dispersed battlefields, there were coincidental developments in C2 capabilities, such as the telegraph, telephone, and radio, which greatly accelerated the rate of transfer of data. The advent of satellite communications and the technology of the information age enabled even faster communications between commanders and subordinates. NCW can accelerate and improve upon that technological trend, but it cannot replace either those who are trained to evaluate and process the data as it moves from node to node, or the decision-maker where the process culminates—the commander.

NCW captures the latest improvements to this incremental development process of technology supporting C2. The technology does speed the information flow and makes it readily available to more users at each level of command. NCW is an enabler of sound leadership, strategy, and application of time-tested doctrinal principles. The Air Force views NCW as a construct that affects an environment, or a broad and enduring concept that has supported effective C2 of military forces throughout their history.

Network-centric operations (NCO) involve the application of elements of NCW to military operations across the full range of military operations. By using a networked system, US forces gain a significant advantage over non-networked forces. This competitive advantage is readily apparent when comparing forces conducting NCO and those operating under the old paradigm of platform-centric operations. Platform-centric forces lack the ability to leverage the synergies created through a networked force. A networked force is more adaptive and ready to respond to future uncertainty at all levels of warfare and across the range of military operations. When considering the most recent combat experience of US forces in Afghanistan and Iraq, it is apparent that platforms retained a central focus, but the networking of those platforms and organizations greatly enhanced their lethality and survivability. Networking enables quicker information transfer and processing, but it also improves the redundancy of information systems by sharing data among all users. If one critical node is disabled, others will have the ability to forward and process that same data, enabling uninterrupted decision-making. Though a networked force has many advantages, it also creates vulnerabilities.

Network warfare operations (NW Ops), are the integrated planning and employment of military capabilities to achieve desired effects across the interconnected analog and digital portion of the operational environment. Network warfare operations are conducted in the information domain through the dynamic combination of hardware, software, data, and human interaction. The operational activities of network warfare operations are network attack (NetA), network defense (NetD) and network warfare support.

Networks include telecommunication devices and data services networks. NetA, a sub-class capability of NW Ops, is conducted to deny, delay, or degrade information resident in networks or processes dependent on those networks,. A primary effect is to reduce an adversary commander's decision-making capability. NetA can contribute effects in support of all air and space power functions and across the range of military operations. One example of NetA employment includes actions taken to reduce adversary's' effectiveness by denying them the use of their networks by affecting the ability of the network to perform its designated function. NetA may support deception operations against an adversary by deleting or distorting information stored on, processed by, or transmitted by network devices. Psychological operations can be performed using NetA to target and disseminate selected information to target audiences. NetA can also offer the commander the ability to incapacitate an adversary while reducing exposure of friendly forces, reducing collateral damage, and saving conventional sorties for other targets.

Network attack, like all other information operations, is most effective and efficient when combined with other air and space operations. Certain aspects of electronic warfare operations overlap NetA and should be coordinated. An example of this is where concurrent physical attack is integrated with NetA and can protect our operations and technology, while exploiting adversarial vulnerabilities. For more on NetA operations and NW Ops see AFDD 2-5, *Information Operations*.

As the network-centric transformation becomes more widespread, we must ensure that our networks are properly designed to ensure protection of information and information systems through information assurance (IA) measures and proper filtering of information at the user's end. Network and information compatibility must be developed and employed if we expect successful joint and coalition operations to achieve a cohesive effort among partners. Finally, as long as current doctrinal tenets such as decentralized execution remain valid, they should guide network development.

Commanders and Staffs

JFCs and Service component commanders at various levels are provided staffs to assist them in the decision-making and execution process. The staff is an extension of the commander. Its sole function is command support, and its only authority is that which is delegated to it by the commander. The staff cannot issue orders to subordinate elements. Orders must be vetted through and issued by the commander, to other commanders, whether in a joint or a Service component chain of command. Staffs may advise and assist in executing operations. **Command may be delegated to another commander, but never to a staff**. A properly trained and directed staff will free the commander to devote more attention to directing subordinate commanders and maintaining a picture of the situation as a whole. The staff should be composed of the smallest number of qualified personnel who can do the job.

The term used to describe the chain of command through which command is exercised is the *command channel*. It is reserved for use by designated commanders. Commanders interact with staffs through the *staff channel*. This is the channel by which staff officers contact their counterparts at higher, adjacent, and subordinate headquarters. These staff-to-staff contacts are for coordination and cooperation only. Higher headquarters staff officers exercise no independent authority over subordinate headquarters staffs, although staff officers normally honor requests for information.

CONSIDERATIONS FOR COMMAND AND CONTROL OPERATIONS

Air Force C2 enables commanders to lead missions within the contextual constraints of policies, resources, and environment. Effective C2 of forces at all levels of conflict and at each level of command, whether strategic, operational, or tactical, requires extensive planning and preparation before operations commence. Requirements for C2 of a force must be intertwined with operations and logistics planning for operations to be effective. Air Force operations are global in nature and require information from around the world to effectively plan and execute missions. Theater systems must be linked to global systems for sharing of information. Some considerations for well-planned C2 support are:

✪ Coverage: The Air Force's C2 system must have adequate coverage with sensors and nodes for intelligence, surveillance, and reconnaissance; weather data; air traffic control; and other capabilities. This system must support contingencies and peacetime operations and the theater commander's as well as supported and supporting commanders' plans and objectives.

✪ Connectivity: Effective C2 of forces relies on global communications to collaborate across domains, to synchronize simultaneous operations in multiple theaters, and to provide global reachback capabilities. The theater C2 system must also provide connectivity to users throughout the theater and sometimes provide reachback capability to supporting C2 and ISR nodes in the continental US and other locations.

✪ Functionality: There should be sufficient redundant decentralized execution nodes for the specific areas of strategic attack, counterair, counterland, air refueling, airspace control, as well as other air and space function mission requirements. These redundant nodes will enable continuity of operations if a senior level command C2 node has been disabled or becomes unable to function in its role.

✪ Placement: Political and geographic constraints may affect C2 system node placement and thus affect the flexibility of its employment. Host nation sensitivities and cultural considerations may not always allow the optimum placement of C2 nodes to enable their maximum capabilities. Planners must take these considerations into account.

Since the details of most C2 operations are not specified by superior commanders, the responsibilities for the details of implied tasks normally fall upon operational and tactical commanders. Commanders should describe their C2 objectives, intent, resources, acceptable risks, and strategies to subordinates. A centralized plan for C2 operations is developed through the iterative campaign planning process as detailed in Air Force and joint publications. The uncertainty of conflict throughout the spectrum of engagement makes the C2 planning process just as important as the C2 section of the contingency plan itself.

US forces may participate in relief operations or homeland operations which require connectivity with civil agencies, host nation forces, or international organizations. When US forces fight as part of a joint or multinational force, responsibilities for C2 operations are by necessity shared among national, functional, and Service component commanders. It is up to the JFC or multinational force commander and staff to determine a workable theater C2 plan. A primary consideration is choosing among parallel, lead nation, or multinational C2 structures. See JP 3-0, *Joint Operations*, for details on these C2 structures. In complex multinational operations, C2 often proves to be the essential mission-enabler, without which effective coalition operations would be impossible.

> A prince or general can best demonstrate his genius by managing a campaign exactly to suit his objectives and his resources, doing neither too much nor too little.
>
> **—Carl von Clausewitz**

MULTINATIONAL AND INTERAGENCY CONSIDERATIONS

Multinational Considerations

US military operations often are conducted with the armed forces of other nations in pursuit of common objectives. Multinational operations, both those that include combat and those that do not, are conducted within the structure of an alliance or coalition. An alliance is a result of formal agreements between two or more nations for broad, long-term objectives (e.g., the North Atlantic Treaty Organization [NATO]). These alliance operations are combined operations, though in common usage combined often is used inappropriately as a synonym for all multinational operations. A coalition is an ad hoc arrangement between two or more nations for common action, for instance the coalition that defeated Iraqi aggression against Kuwait in Operation DESERT STORM. Joint operations as part of an alliance or coalition require close cooperation among all forces and can serve to mass strengths, reduce vulnerabilities, and provide legitimacy. Effectively planned and executed multinational operations should, in addition to achieving common objectives, facilitate unity of effort without diminishing freedom of action and preserve unit integrity and uninterrupted support.

Each multinational operation is unique, and key considerations involved in planning and conducting multinational operations vary with the international situation and perspectives, motives, and values of the organization's members. Whereas alliance members typically have common national political and economic systems, coalitions often bring together nations of diverse cultures for a limited period of time. As long as the coalition members perceive their membership and participation as advancing their individual national interests, the coalition can remain intact. At the point that national objectives or priorities diverge, the coalition strains to function or breaks down.

The armed forces of the United States should be prepared to operate within the framework of an alliance or coalition under other-than-US leadership. Following, contributing, and supporting are important roles in multinational operations—often as important as leading. However, US forces often will be the predominant and most capable force within an alliance or coalition and can be expected to play a central leadership role, albeit one founded on mutual respect. Stakes are high, requiring the military leaders of member nations to emphasize common objectives as well as mutual support and respect. For additional guidance on multinational operations, refer to JP 3-0, and JP 3-16, *Joint Doctrine for Multinational Operations.*

Interagency Considerations

Interagency coordination forges the vital link between the military and the economic, diplomatic, and informational entities of the US government as well as non-governmental organizations (NGOs) and international organizations (IOs). Successful interagency coordination and planning enable these agencies, departments, and organizations to mount a coherent and efficient collective operation to achieve unity of effort.

Across the range of military operations, a broad variety of agencies, many with indispensable practical competencies and major legal responsibilities, interact with the armed forces of the United States. *Obtaining coordinated and integrated effort in an interagency operation should not be equated to the C2 of a military operation.* Various agencies' different and sometimes conflicting goals, policies, procedures, and decision-making techniques make unity of effort a challenge.

OPERATIONAL RISK MANAGEMENT

Risk management is part of the commander's responsibility and should be involved in his/her decision-making process. Commanders should assess and accept risks necessary to accomplish the mission. Accepting risks also acknowledges the possibility of failure. Assessing risks may be a time-consuming process; however, not assessing risks turns the decision-making process into a dangerous gamble. Commanders should take advantage of vertical and horizontal information fusion efforts to optimize timely and informed decision making. Effective operational risk management principles must be employed before, during, and after military operations to prevent mishaps. Commanders must advocate and employ proactive mishap prevention principles to prosecute military operations safely and effectively. For information on operational risk management, see AFI 90-901, *Operational Risk Management*, and Air Force Tactics, Techniques, and Procedures (Inter-Service) (AFTTP[I]) 3–2.34, *Multiservice Tactics, Techniques and Procedures for Risk Management.*

Case Study: The Challenges of Network-Centric C2

Operation ANACONDA: Afghanistan, April 2002

... [There] was frustration over failing to hit a truck observed on Predator video. Watching a live Predator feed, the JOC at Bagram spotted a truck behind the battle lines that appeared to be resupplying enemy forces and ordered it killed. CJTF Mountain told the ASOC cell to blow up the truck. The ASOC told him they had troops-in-contact requests but he reiterated the order. "We tried to send several sets of fighters at it," the Assistant Division ALO attested. As he told the story two months later: ...this truck was a flatbed, stake-bed truck driving through a ravine up in the hills, in the vicinity of but not in the heat of battle...the first aircraft they sent over there were F-16s and ... they couldn't find them so they ran out of gas. Everybody is tensely awaiting to see this thing blow up on TV. ...We had another set of F-18s, sent them in, bottom line, never hit it.... This story, recalled from the heat of battle, vividly conveyed the sense of frustration with the air control system and uncertainty over the rules of engagement. The truck was difficult to find without a FAC in place to pass along the coordinates and help talk the aircraft onto the target. Frustration aside, the fundamental issue remained about the propriety of diverting strike assets from troops-in-contact to chase a truck. He summarized that the Predator's live feed "stared at that truck for hours ...It was a waste of an asset that could have helped defend guys, could have helped with other targeting." The dramatic failure to hit the truck was carried out in clear view, because of the live Predator feed to the JOC.

—Operation ANACONDA, An Airpower Perspective;
The Office of Air Force Lessons Learned
Task Force Enduring Look

This example illustrates the challenges presented by the advanced information capabilities offered up to commanders by technology. While the flatbed truck was a target that was readily available, had it not been presented to the entire staff by the Predator feed, it would not have generated the interest that it did. In fact, it diverted the commander's attention from the targets that were more important—troops in contact.

Today's technology allows commanders to view some, but not all, aspects of a conflict. It is important for commanders at all levels, but especially at the operational and strategic level, not to become fixated on one target or incident they can view through advances in technology. The concepts of centralized control and decentralized execution must still be observed, to allow subordinates to execute and to avoid "target fixation" at senior levels.

CHAPTER TWO

AIR FORCE C2 IN THE ADMINISTRATIVE CHAIN OF COMMAND

Effective C2... allows our forces to control what moves through air and space; engage adversary targets anywhere, anytime; control and exploit information to our nation's advantage; deliver desirable effects with acceptable risk and minimal collateral damage; rapidly position forces anywhere in the world; and sustain flexible and effective combat operations.

—General Michael E. Ryan,
Chief of Staff, United States Air Force (CSAF), 1997-2001

ADMINISTRATIVE VERSUS OPERATIONAL C2 ENVIRONMENT

The US Constitution provides for civilian control of the military. This civilian control is provided by the President and the SecDef. The UNAAF presents the chain of command for both administrative and operational control of the armed forces. The President and the SecDef exercise authority and control of the armed forces through two distinct branches of the chain of command. One branch runs from the President, through the SecDef, directly to the commanders of combatant commands for missions and forces assigned to their commands. This is commonly referred to as the "operational" chain of command. The other branch, (commonly referred to as the "administrative" chain of command) is used for purposes other than operational direction of forces assigned to combatant commands. It runs from the President, through the SecDef, to the Secretaries of the military departments. The military departments, organized separately, operate under the authority, direction, and control of the SecDef. The Secretaries of the military departments exercise authority through their respective Service chiefs over their forces not assigned to the combatant commanders. See Figure 2.1 for a representation of the operational and administrative chains of command and control as they apply to US forces, including Air Force forces. For more on the chain of command and control of US forces see JP 0-2.

One way to differentiate between functions and missions, and to understand the two distinct branches of the chain of command is to distinguish between the functions a Service performs under the auspices of the administrative branch of the chain of command and those functions provided to a joint force commander via the operational branch of the chain of command. Along these lines, it is useful to make a distinction between "administrative and organizational functions" (those activities required to develop and sustain the Air Force as a corporate entity) and "operational functions" (those warfighting activities involving the application of air and space power to achieve specific military effects). The way that forces are employed, and thus commanded, is guided by whether those forces fall under the operational or the administrative functions of the DOD. This also guides the command arrangements and relationships and dictates the C2 structure for these forces.

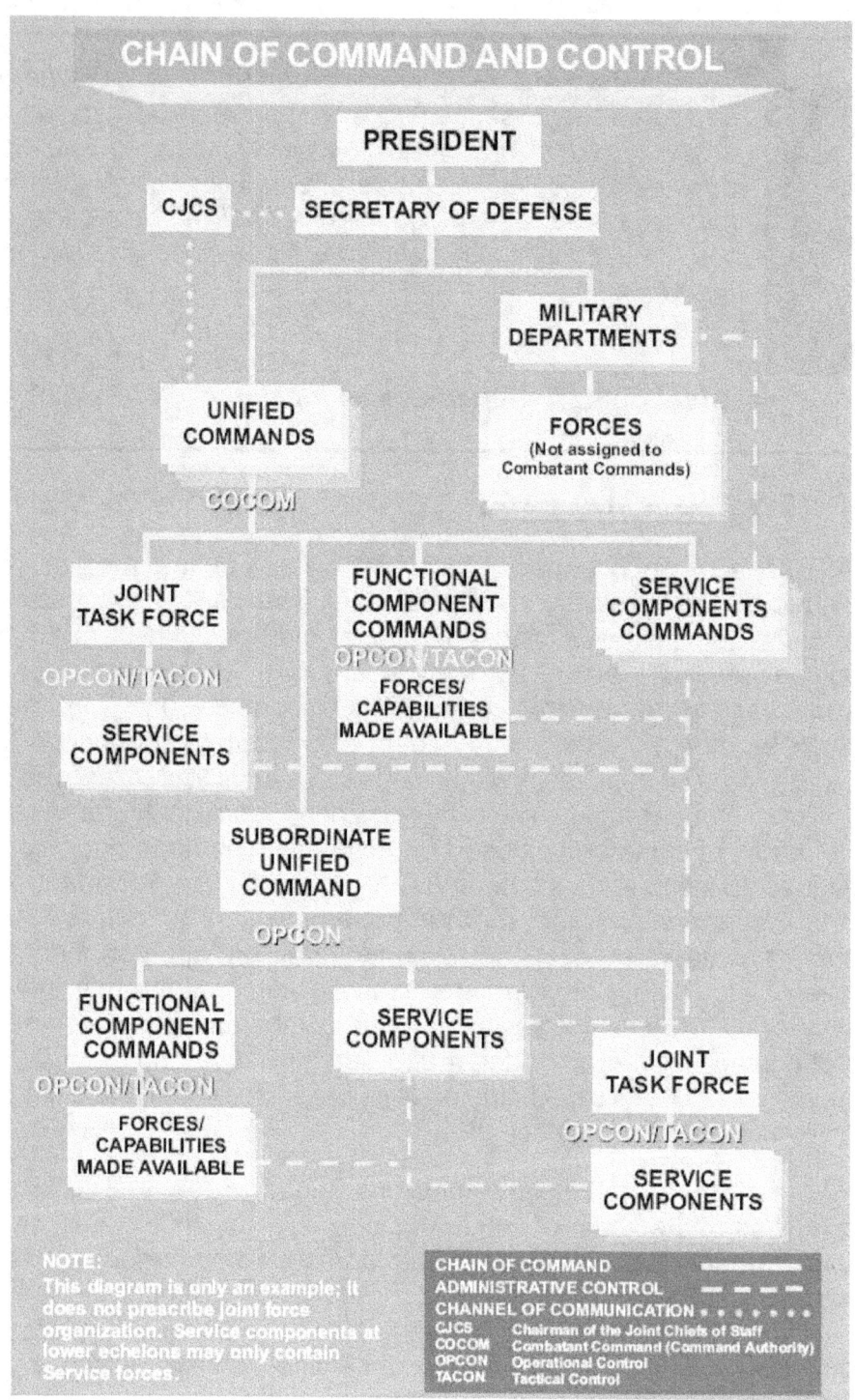

Figure 2.1. The Chain of Command and Control for US Forces.

COMMAND RELATIONSHIPS AND LEVELS OF AUTHORITY

There are varying levels of authority and different command relationships governing forces that fall under the operational chain of command or the administrative chain. Forces fall under the administrative control of the Secretaries of the military departments until they are presented to combatant commanders for employment. Once they are presented to the combatant commander, they fall under the operational chain of command.

Combatant commanders employ forces, in contrast to the Service chiefs, who are tasked by law to organize, train, and equip US military forces. These differing responsibilities require different command relationships and levels of authority to accomplish designated roles and missions.

The authority vested in a commander must be commensurate with the responsibility assigned. Levels of authority vary, depending upon the type of command relationship involved. Combatant commanders exercise combatant command (COCOM) over assigned forces and are directly responsible to the President and SecDef for the performance of assigned missions and the preparedness of their commands to perform assigned missions. COCOM is nontransferable and cannot be delegated. Operational control (OPCON) is inherent in COCOM and is the authority to perform those functions of command over subordinate forces involving organizing and employing commands and forces, assigning tasks, designating objectives, and giving authoritative direction necessary to accomplish the mission. OPCON includes authoritative direction over all aspects of military operations and joint training necessary to accomplish missions assigned to the command. OPCON may be delegated within the command. Tactical control (TACON) is the command authority over assigned or attached forces or commands or military capability made available for tasking that is limited to the detailed direction and control of movements or maneuvers within the operational area necessary to accomplish assigned missions or tasks. TACON is inherent in OPCON and may be delegated to and exercised by commanders at any echelon at or below the level of combatant command.

Support is a command authority. A support relationship is established by a superior commander between subordinate commanders when one organization should aid, protect, complement, or sustain another force. Support may be exercised by commanders at any echelon at or below the level of combatant command. Several categories of support have been defined for use within a combatant command as appropriate to better characterize the support that should be given. Support relationships may be categorized as general, mutual, direct, and close.

Modern information technology systems afford air and space commanders with vastly improved information resources that improve situational awareness and understanding and may help reduce forward-deployed footprints. These same information resources have an inherent capability to provide undue rear area influence in the engaged commander's C2 process. In light of this development, it is critical that supported/supporting relationships are clearly understood by commanders and their staffs.

Other authorities critical to C2 operations are administrative control (ADCON), coordinating authority, and direct liaison authorized (DIRLAUTH). Commanders must thoroughly understand command authorities and the concept of command relationships, as this area could well be a source of confusion. See Appendix A for a listing and description of command authorities. For a brief description of the levels of authority and command relationships, see Appendix A, and AFDD 2, *Operations and Organization*.

Derivation of Command Relationships

The relationships between combatant commanders or commanders within a JTF and between JTFs are prescribed by law and are based on proven doctrinal precepts. The SecDef is the only authority who can transfer forces between combatant commands. A request for transfer of forces is initiated by the requesting commander and forwarded to the joint staff for action, resulting in either approval or disapproval by the SecDef. The SecDef gives direction to the joint chiefs for the operational employment of US forces.

Once direction is given from the President and the SecDef, JFCs use command (the lawful authority of a commander) and control (the regulation of forces and functions) to accomplish the mission in accordance with the commander's intent (or President and the SecDef's intent). This is the most important function undertaken by a JFC. C2 is the means by which a JFC synchronizes and integrates joint force activities in order to achieve unity of command and unity of effort. C2 ties together all the operational functions and tasks and applies to all levels of war and echelons of command across the range of military operations. C2 of joint operations begins by establishing unity of command through the designation of a JFC with the requisite authority to accomplish assigned tasks using an uncomplicated chain of command. It is essential for the JFC to ensure that subordinate commanders, staff principals, and leaders of C2 nodes understand their authorities, their role in decision making and controlling, and their relationships with others.

The JFC organizes assigned and attached forces to accomplish the mission based on their vision and concept of operations as well as planning considerations and the requirements of the AOR. Unity of effort, centralized planning and direction, and decentralized execution are also key considerations. JFCs can conduct operations through subordinate JTFs, Service components, functional components, or a combination of Service and functional components. The JFC establishes subordinate commands, assigns responsibilities, establishes or delegates appropriate command relationships, and establishes coordinating instructions for the component commanders.

The JFC establishes the command and supported/supporting relationships and assignment of forces to accomplish mission objectives. The JFC will also specify the command relationships between the functional components and Service components.

OPCON and TACON are normally employed by the JFC to control forces, with each AOR being situation- and scenario-dependent for the command structure.

Presentation of Forces

Forces (except as noted in Title 10, US Code [U.S.C.], section 162) are assigned to combatant commands by the SecDef's "Forces for Unified Commands" memorandum. A force assigned or attached to a combatant command may be transferred from that command only as directed by the SecDef and under procedures prescribed by the SecDef and approved by the President. The command relationship the gaining commander will exercise (and the losing commander will relinquish) will be specified by the SecDef. Establishing authorities for subordinate unified commands and JTFs may direct the assignment or attachment of their forces to those subordinate commands as appropriate. When forces are transferred between combatant commands, the command relationship the gaining commander will exercise over those forces must be specified by the SecDef.

Attachment of Air Force Forces to Combatant Commands

Air Force forces are presented to joint force commanders in a single, capabilities-based entity—the air and space expeditionary task force (AETF). The AETF consists of fielded forces, a COMAFFOR, and appropriate C2 mechanisms (an AOC and an AFFOR Staff). The AFFOR Staff is tailored to meet specific mission requirements. It supports the COMAFFOR as the senior operational-level component warfighter with established OPCON and ADCON of assigned/attached Air Force forces. When aligned to support a geographic combatant commander, the AFFOR Staff provides a capable, ready, and theater-smart C2 element for the COMAFFOR. *Regardless of the size of the Air Force element, it will be organized along the lines of an AETF.*

Air Force Capabilities Not Assigned to Combatant Commands

There are Air Force organizations capable of being tasked to support military operations that are not assigned to combatant commands. These organizations exist primarily within the Air Force's administrative chain of command. They are not as visible for tasking and deployment, although their functions may support continuous military operations through a variety of intelligence, support, and logistics functions, for example. These organizations may deploy personnel forward or support operations in place, using the concept of reachback. They may be made up of a combination of Airmen (using the total force concept) and contractor personnel. Their relationships with the COMAFFOR may be governed by formal command relationships such as a supporting/supported relationship or by memorandum of agreement/understanding or formal contract. Depending on how they will be integrated and employed (deployed or in-place support), the COMAFFOR requests Air Force forces through their combatant commander, the Secretary of the Air Force (SECAF) (for those Air Force forces not assigned to combatant commands), and the President/SecDef. For a representative sample of agencies that remain in the administrative chain of command but also provide support to the COMAFFOR, see Figure 2.2.

Examples of Air Force Organizations not Assigned to Combatant Commands	
Organization	Capability
Air Force Agency for Modeling and Simulation	Conducts modeling and simulation programs and initiatives.
Air National Guard Readiness Center	Provides information to forces providing contingency augmentation.
Any Air Staff DCS or Directorate or MAJCOM as required	Provides policy, guidance, and oversight for Air Force FOAs, DRUs, and functional area expertise of organic Air Force capabilities.
Air Force Audit Agency	Audits for efficiency and effectiveness.
Air Force Civil Engineering Support Agency	Provides the best tools, practices, and professional support for base-level and contingency operations.
Air Force Communications Agency	Provides communications expertise and services.
Air Force Doctrine Center	Focal point for air and space doctrine support to warfighters.
Air Force Flight Standards Agency	Performs worldwide flight inspections of airfields and flight instrumentation/navigation systems.
Air Intelligence Agency	Provides intelligence expertise in the areas of C2 protection, security, acquisition, foreign weapons systems and technology, and treaty monitoring.
Air Force Legal Operations Agency	Provides commanders with specialized legal services.
Air Force Logistics Management Agency	Develops, analyzes, tests, evaluates, and recommends new or improved logistical procedures.
Air Force Medical Operations Agency	Develops programs to improve aerospace medicine and preventive and clinical healthcare services.

Figure 2.2. Examples of Air Force Organizations not Assigned to Combatant Commands.

The Air Intelligence Agency (AIA) executes missions assigned by the National Security Agency (NSA), the Defense Intelligence Agency (DIA), and the Air Force. Their unique, by-law arrangements allow the organization to support the Service chief, the Joint Chiefs of Staff (JCS), and the nation's senior defense policymakers. In contrast, most other C2 facilities support either the civilian or military chains of command. The AIA offers support to the JFCs at USSTRATCOM and US Joint Forces Command (USJFCOM). The AIA falls under the ADCON of Air Combat Command (ACC). However, its cryptologic collection management authority flows from the NSA, reflecting its unique command arrangement, which gives the commander OPCON over all cryptologic activity conducted anywhere in the Air Force.

Some agencies, such as the AIA, have a unique command arrangement, established by laws contained in Title 10 and Title 50, U.S.C. These "dual-purpose" military forces are funded and controlled by organizations that derive authority under laws contained in both Title 10 and Title 50. The greatest benefit of these "dual-purpose" forces is their authority to operate under laws contained in Title 50, and so produce actionable intelligence products and information, while being employed by combatant commanders. These forces are primarily organized, trained, and equipped under Title 10. They serve both the military chain of command and the nation's senior defense policymakers.

Organization of Functional Forces

Some operational forces are organized functionally. Some air and space forces employed in an operation will not be attached forward to a geographic combatant commander. Several aspects of air and space power are capable of serving more than one geographic combatant commander at a time and thus require optimization above the theater level. Such capabilities—air mobility, space, and special operations forces (SOF)—are instead organized under functional combatant commanders who normally retain control of such forces. Although functional forces may be transferred to a geographic combatant commander (with specification of OPCON or TACON), *the preferred command relationship between geographic combatant commands and functional organizations not assigned or attached to the geographic combatant command is support.* For theater air mobility, this support relationship is normally facilitated through a specially designated representative, attached to regional AETFs; the director of air mobility forces (DIRMOBFOR-AIR), *who is responsible for integrating the total air mobility effort for the CFACC.* Similarly, the director of space forces (DIRSPACEFOR) is the senior space operations advisor to the COMAFFOR.

THE ADMINISTRATIVE BRANCH

Administrative Control

The authority vested in the Secretaries of the military departments in the performance of their role to organize, train, equip, and provide forces runs from the President through the SecDef to the Secretaries. This authority is reflected in Title 10, U.S.C. Then, to the degree established by the Secretaries or specified in law, this authority runs through the Service chiefs to the Service component commanders assigned to the combatant commands and to the commanders of forces not assigned to the combatant commands. This ADCON provides for the preparation of military forces and their administration and support, unless such responsibilities are specifically assigned by the SecDef to another DOD component. For more information on the functions of the Air Force, see DOD Directive (DODD) 5100.1, *Functions of the Department of Defense and Its Components.*

ADCON is defined in JP 1-02 as the direction or exercise of authority over subordinate or other organizations in respect to administration and support, including organization of Service forces, control of resources and equipment, personnel management, unit logistics, individual and unit training, readiness, mobilization, demobilization, discipline, and other matters not included in the operational missions of the subordinate or other organizations.

ADCON is the authority necessary to fulfill military department statutory responsibilities for administration and support. The Chief of Staff of the Air Force and every other Air Force commander use ADCON authority to organize, train, and equip Air Force forces to be ready to meet contingencies and to carry out the orders of the President and the SecDef. Providing for the welfare of all Airmen is one of the responsibilities of ADCON. The Air Force has a set of C2 nodes that support commanders in their functions to prepare, train, and equip Airmen for possible contingencies. These nodes are primarily fixed, but some also have a mobile or deployable capability. They are usually configured to support both the ADCON responsibilities of their commander, as well as any operational requirements, such as mobilizing to meet a commander's tasking.

Responsibilities of the COMAFFOR: Administrative and Operational

The COMAFFOR commands forces through two separate chains of responsibilities, the administrative and the operational. The operational chain runs through joint channels from the JFC and is expressed in terms such as OPCON, TACON, and support. The administrative chain runs through Service channels only, from the AETF, up through the regional major command (MAJCOM) (if present), to the CSAF and SECAF. This authority is expressed as ADCON.

The COMAFFOR is the Air Force officer designated as commander of the Air Force component command assigned or attached to a JFC at the unified, subunified, and JTF level, or as commander of a single Service task force. C2 of Air Force forces assigned or attached to the Air Force component is exercised through the COMAFFOR. Air Force forces should be organized as an AETF, whose commander is the COMAFFOR. Through the JFC's command authority, the JFC normally will conduct operations through the COMAFFOR by delegating OPCON of the Air Force component forces to the COMAFFOR. When designated as the CFACC, the COMAFFOR normally maintains OPCON of assigned and attached Air Force forces and normally receives TACON of forces from other Service or functional components as directed by the JFC. If the CFACC is designated from another component of the joint force, the COMAFFOR will ensure Air Force forces are employed in accordance with the CFACC's guidance and tasking. If the CFACC is designated from another component of the joint force, the COMAFFOR still retains OPCON and ADCON of Air Force forces. Only TACON is passed to the CFACC, whether or not the COMAFFOR is dual-hatted as the CFACC. The administrative responsibilities of the COMAFFOR are discussed below. His/her operational responsibilities are discussed in chapter three.

Administrative (Service) Responsibilities of the COMAFFOR

Commanders of Air Force components have responsibilities and authorities that derive from their roles in fulfilling the Service's ADCON function under Title 10, U.S.C.

Through the JFC's command authority, the JFC normally will conduct operations through the COMAFFOR by delegating OPCON of the Air Force component forces to the COMAFFOR. Through the Service's ADCON authority, the COMAFFOR will have complete ADCON of all assigned Air Force component forces and specified ADCON of all attached Air Force component forces. The specified ADCON responsibilities apply to all attached forces, regardless of MAJCOM or Air Force component (regular, Guard, or Reserve). The COMAFFOR also has some ADCON responsibilities for Air Force elements and personnel assigned to other joint force components (such as liaisons). The Air National Guard (ANG) and Air Force Reserve Command (AFRC) retain all other ADCON responsibilities, such as Reserve component activation, deactivation, partial mobilization, and length of tour. Additionally, intertheater forces, such as intertheater airlift and forces transiting another COMAFFOR's area of interest, will be subject to the ADCON authority of the respective COMAFFOR while transiting that COMAFFOR's area only for administrative reporting and for TACON for force protection requirements derived from the combatant commander. For more on this relationship see AFDD 2, *Organization and Operations.*

G-series orders are the means used to activate, inactivate, redesignate, assign, and reassign units and detachments subordinate to a MAJCOM, field operating agency (FOA), or direct reporting unit (DRU); and to attach one unit to another. A MAJCOM, FOA, or DRU manpower and organization function may authenticate and publish G-series orders. These orders are used to establish clear lines of authority for a COMAFFOR when units from another organization or different organizations are placed within an AETF. See Figure 2.3 for a sample G-series order.

> *ANG assets can be classified into three categories within the law and, with the exception of one very limited situation under 32 U.S.C. §325 requiring approval of the President, can only be in one status at a time. The first is familiar: Title 10, where forces are under the authority of the President as commander in chief. The second category is "state active duty" for ANG forces under the authority of the state governor through the respective state's adjutant general and funded by the state. The third category is Title 32 status. They are under the authority of the state governor for training purposes but funding is from the federal government. The ANG and Air Force have agreed that the joint definition of 'coordinating authority' allows the state governor to direct ANG forces to respond to the direction of a Title 10 commander. The forces are still under the command authority of the governor, but for unity of effort the Title 10 commander (i.e., active duty officer) can direct their actions. However, ANG forces in Title 32 status can only perform training and other specified activities, and have different systems for discipline, union rights, and other areas, so employment details should be planned in advance.*
>
> **—Information derived from Titles 10 and 32, U.S.C.**

DEPARTMENT OF THE AIR FORCE
HEADQUARTERS AIR COMBAT COMMAND
LANGLEY AIR FORCE BASE, VIRGINIA 23665-2778

SPECIAL ORDER
GXXX-XX   DATE

1. (   ) Effective the date of this order, HQ 345th Air Expeditionary Wing (AEW), a provisional unit, is activated at Location, Country, and assigned to the XXth Air and Space Expeditionary Task Force. (XX AETF – [Operation Name]) for the purposes of specified ADCON to include: making recommendations to the COMAFFOR on the proper employment of subordinate units; accomplishing assigned tasks; organizing, training, equipping and sustaining assigned and attached forces; reachback to the US Air Force rear and supporting US Air Force units; force protection; morale, welfare and discipline; and personnel management.

2. (   ) Effective the date of this order, the following units are activated at Location, Country, and assigned as indicated for the purposes of command and control and administrative support:

UNIT	ASSIGNMENT
HQ 345th Expeditionary Operations Group (EOG)	345 AEW
345th Expeditionary Operations Support Squadron	345 EOG
1st Expeditionary Fighter Squadron	345 EOG
HQ 345th Expeditionary Maintenance Group (EMG)	345 AEW
345th Expeditionary Maintenance Operations Squadron	345 EMG
345th Expeditionary Security Forces Squadron	345 EMSG
345th Expeditionary Medical Operations Squadron	345 AEW

3. (   ) Upon Inactivation, the units will permanently retain any honors gained while active as provisional units.

4. (   ) Authority: AFI 38-101, DAF XXXs

FOR THE COMMANDER

DISTRIBUTION:
HQ USAF/DPMO
AFHRA/RS
All units mentioned in order
Others as needed

Classified by:
Dated:
Declassify on:

Figure 2.3. Sample G-Series Order Establishing a Provisional Unit.

G-series orders should detail which commanders are responsible for providing specific elements of specified ADCON to deployed units and what authority that commander may use to carry out these responsibilities (see AFDD 2 and AFI 38-101, *Air Force Organization*, for discussion and examples of G-series orders). The orders are not required to spell out all support and sustainment responsibilities. For a notional example, the orders might specify that lodging, dining, and force protection will be provided by the 36th Air Expeditionary Wing (AEW) from Pacific Air Forces (PACAF). The minimum ADCON responsibilities and authorities to go forward should be responsibility for Uniform Code of Military Justice (UCMJ) actions, protection of assigned forces and assets, lodging, dining, and force reporting.

C2 OF AIR FORCE FORCES

The COMAFFOR requires the ability to provide command and oversight of Air Force forces offered up to the joint or combined operation (i.e., an AOC and an A- staff). Networked, adaptive C2 facilitates integration of the COMAFFOR with warfighting functions to optimize the commanders' ability to execute the military operation. Effective C2 of Air Force forces enables the commander to employ capabilities and resources effectively for mission accomplishment. The COMAFFOR's C2 system should be interoperable, horizontally integrated across functions, vertically integrated across all echelons of command, and provide organizational connectivity between commanders and decision makers down to the employing units.

AFFOR Staff Organization

The primary emphasis of command relationships is to keep the chain of command simple so all involved understand who is in charge. The COMAFFOR will have a dedicated staff to coordinate actions required to accomplish the mission. This is known as the "A" staff. The AFFOR staff assists the COMAFFOR in the decision-making and execution process for Service support and command matters. An extension of the commander, it performs primary functions to support the COMAFFOR and subordinate AETF units. Authorities held by members of the AFFOR staff are only those specifically delegated by the commander. These authorities are clearly communicated, universally understood, and documented for proper accountability in performance of duty. A properly trained and directed staff is absolutely necessary to free the commander to devote requisite attention to command-level matters. Functions common to all staff sections include providing information and advice, making estimates, making recommendations, preparing plans and orders, advising other staffs and subordinate commands of the commander's plans and policies, and supervising the execution of plans and orders. The COMAFFOR and his/her staff should be considered a single entity. Staff officers may be authorized to act in the name of the commander in certain matters; however, no staff officer has any authority over any subordinate unit of the command.

The AFFOR staff normally includes divisions for manpower and personnel, intelligence, operations, logistics, plans, and communications and information and are designated A-1 through A-6 respectively. Other (A-x) designations and functions are also used but they can vary from MAJCOM to MAJCOM (e.g., engineers; analysis, and assessment functions). The staff also includes the personal and special staffs of the COMAFFOR.

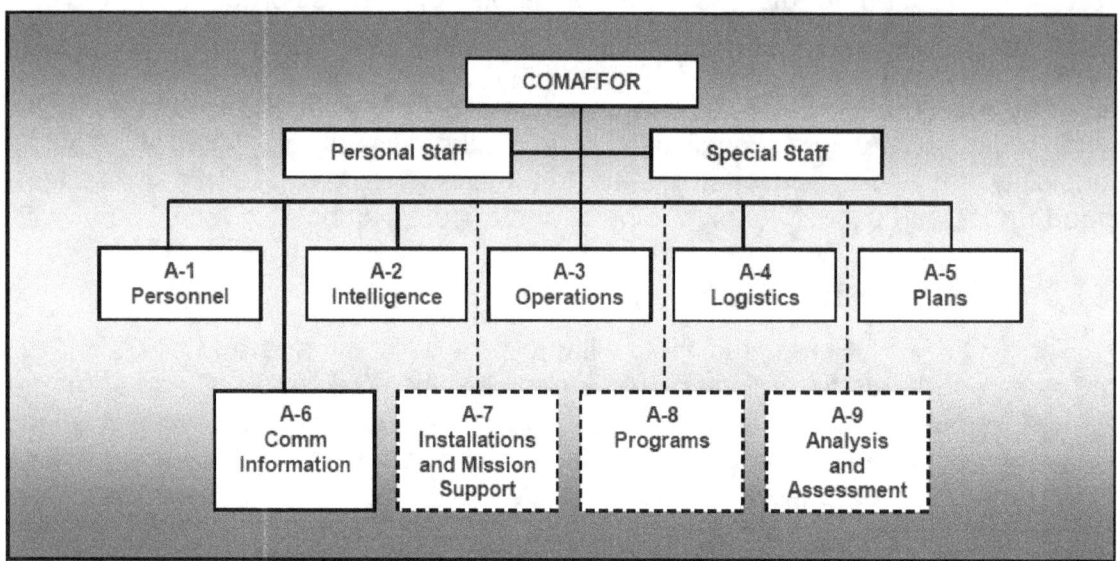

Figure 2.4. Notional A-staff organization

The AFFOR Staff must be able to transition from peacetime to contingency operations. During day-to-day operations, MAJCOM/numbered Air Force (NAF) functions generally fall into two broad categories: Title 10 management tasks and component/AFFOR staff functions. In the transition to contingency operations, the MAJCOM/NAF's component/AFFOR staff becomes the core of the COMAFFOR's staff, rolling in on top of whatever contingency staff may already exist in the theater of operations, as shown in figure 2.4. Augmenting that staff, in priority order, are the non-engaged NAF staffs, the engaged MAJCOM staff, and the non-engaged MAJCOMs. MAJCOMs must pre-identify personnel to fill the AFFOR staff positions.

The AFFOR staff is one vehicle through which the COMAFFOR fulfills his/her operational and administrative responsibilities for assigned and attached forces (the other is the AOC), and is responsible for the long-range planning that occurs outside the air tasking cycle (e.g., contingency planning). The AFFOR staff also has responsibilities to interface with host nation and coalition nations to support contingencies. The COMAFFOR (who may also be the JFACC) may issue traditional mission-type orders to direct subordinate units to execute actions outside the scope of the ATO. Two examples of such orders include setting a baseline force protection condition or directing the move of a unit to another operating base. The AFFOR staff should develop a habitual working relationship with the AOC to help fulfill the COMAFFOR's full range of responsibilities. The AFFOR staff is not the AOC staff. Although some functions may seem to overlap between the staffs, the two organizations should not be "dual hatted" with the same personnel, except in extreme circumstances. Dual hatting will result in the staff members becoming overtasked and having conflicting taskings.

The following discussion of AFFOR staff duties is not intended to be all-inclusive. The differing mission requirements of any given AETF may dictate different task emphasis and staff arrangements. Very large or complex operations, for example, may require all staff directorates. In some cases, senior component liaison elements may not be needed. Some of the required support may be obtained through reachback. For very small or limited operations, a full AFFOR staff may not be required. As a rule of thumb, the size and span of the AFFOR staff should normally be held to the smallest number of divisions necessary to handle the demands of the operation. For example, for a very small, forward deployed operation, the AFFOR staff may consist of only A-1 through A-6; for support of major, theater-wide operations all nine directorates (A-1 through A-9) may be required. For additional information see Air Force Operational Tactics, Techniques, and Procedures (AFOTTP) 2-3.3, *Air Force Forces.*

The COMAFFOR may elect to send liaisons to other components or to a joint force headquarters. The Air Force liaison element (AFLE) provides an interface between the COMAFFOR and component commanders for coordinating and synchronizing Air Force units in support of joint air operations. Normally, the AFLE is composed of personnel and equipment for a general purpose numbered Air Force's staff and component organizations. AFLE manning is based on a cadre concept with personnel selected for their battle management expertise and knowledge of C2 concepts and procedures. The cadres are augmented by additional personnel who are specialists knowledgeable in the capabilities and tactics of the aircraft, intelligence, or weapons systems being employed. The AFLE can be tailored to perform a variety of missions and management functions to match the contingency or operation.

Combat Support C2

Combat support C2 (CSC2) enables the commander to employ capabilities and resources effectively (despite competing demands). It also provides the means for implementing combat support plans, and the agility to modify those plans as necessary to meet evolving operational requirements. For more information on CSC2, see AFDD 2-4, *Combat Support.*

Networked, adaptive, and integrated CSC2 facilitates integration with warfighting functions. It is required to maximize C2 planning and tasking efforts and to optimize the commanders' ability to control and execute the military operation. CSC2 supports the mission and provides input to operational risk mitigation, near-real time CSC2 information, and cross-AOR resource planning and arbitration. The key to operational risk mitigation is the integration of Air Force C2 centers at all levels, sustaining base and agile combat support (ACS) capabilities for global and theater missions and resource optimization. Additionally, near-real time dynamic, continuous management of C2 and combat support/operational intelligence ensures adaptive operations and effective combat support plans.

The COMAFFOR requires the ability to maintain awareness of the status of the friendly forces order of battle, recognize what support capability is needed where, and direct resources accordingly. Many Air Force resources are limited and designed to serve the needs of multiple missions in widely dispersed unified commands. Centralized control and decentralized execution of these resources are especially critical to assure an optimum balance between flexibility and responsiveness of Air Force combat support. Key to this is the concept that various echelons need visibility and authority over assets relevant to their respective roles and responsibilities.

CSC2 Processes and Capabilities

CSC2 uses the monitor, assess, plan, and execute (MAPE) process. The inherent capabilities of this process allow commanders to employ combat support capabilities and resources effectively. CSC2 systems provide the tools and technology to access, analyze, display, and act upon relevant information enabling them to ready, deploy, employ, and sustain forces for assigned missions worldwide. These capabilities and processes bring into focus the continuum of action required to link operational and combat support capabilities to achieve desired effects.

Full range planning and execution of Air Force forces require an ACS C2 architecture that is integrated across the functional areas of combat support and provides secure and nonsecure capability. Connectivity to any deployed operating location, including bare bases, is needed early; robust secure communications and information capabilities should connect all combat support functions.

Combat Support Organization and Commanders' Roles and Responsibilities

Combatant commanders exercise COCOM and directive authority for logistics. For assigned Air Force forces, they exercise their authority through the COMAFFOR who is normally dual-hatted as the CFACC. Additionally, when United States Transportation Command (USTRANSCOM) is supporting a geographic combatant commander with airlift and air refueling capabilities, the CFACC normally provides the majority of C2 interface for those assets. Air Force C2 structures for combat support are designed to enable a COMAFFOR's ability to support the combatant commander's exercise of his/her directive authority for logistics.

When MAJCOMs are the combatant command's Air Force component, they advise how to organize and employ these forces to accomplish assigned missions. MAJCOMs, in their role as the theater AFFOR, provide theater reachback support to the regional AFFOR. NAFs provide the senior Air Force warfighting echelon and provide the organizational combat support planning expertise. The NAF staff plans the C2 architecture for operations and forms the core of the regional AFFOR staff. Air Force commanders should be prepared to accept single-Service responsibility for joint common use items. Regardless of the source of support or support C2 structure, the Service component is responsible for ensuring essential combat support for assigned or attached Air Force forces within a joint command.

Joint Task Forces Katrina Lessons Learned

One of the lessons learned from DOD support to civil operations supporting Hurricane Katrina involved the C2 of active duty and reserve forces providing relief. *The Federal Response to Hurricane Katrina, Lessons Learned* stated: "A fragmented deployment system and lack of an integrated command structure for both active duty and National Guard forces exacerbated communications and coordination issues during the initial response. Deployments for Title 32 (National Guard) forces were coordinated State-to-State through Emergency Management Assistance Compact agreements and also by the National Guard Bureau. Title 10 (active duty) force deployments were coordinated through USNORTHCOM. Once forces arrived in the Joint Operations Area, they fell under separate command structures, rather than one single command. The separate commands divided the area of operations geographically and supported response efforts separately, with the exception of the evacuations of the Superdome and the Convention Center in New Orleans. Equipment interoperability problems further hindered an integrated response. Similar issues of bifurcated operations and interoperability challenges were also present between the military and civilian leadership…".

LESSON LEARNED: The Departments of Homeland Security and Defense should jointly plan for the Department of Defense's support of Federal response activities as well as those extraordinary circumstances when it is appropriate for the Department of Defense to lead the Federal response. In addition, the Department of Defense should ensure the transformation of the National Guard is focused on increased integration with active duty forces for homeland security plans and activities.

—The Federal Response to Hurricane Katrina, Lessons Learned

The Senior/Host Air Force Installation Commander

An Installation commander, regardless of Service, always exercises responsibility for forces on his/her base for protection of assigned forces and assets, and for other base operations support-integration (BOS-I) functions such as dining and lodging regardless of the command relations of those forces. These are the inherent responsibilities of an installation commander.

Ultimately, the Air Force Service component commander within a region is responsible for fulfilling ADCON responsibilities and common logistics support for all Air Force forces within his/her region, regardless of organization or assignment of those forces. These ADCON responsibilities are exercised through commanders at subordinate echelons. The ADCON chain is clear for non-deployed forces at home station during peacetime. However, the ADCON chain during expeditionary operations requires some fundamental guidance, especially during those fluid times when forces are initially building up in remote deployed locations. The senior Air Force commander on any base where Air Force forces are present has responsibilities for care and provisioning of the Air Force forces on that installation, regardless of organization. See AFDD 2, *Operations and Organization,* for more on the ADCON responsibilities of the senior/host installation commander.

The Senior Airfield Authority

The ability to open and establish airbases is a key enabler facilitating both strategic and operational reach across the range of military operations. To alleviate C2 issues and mitigate concerns about airfield authority, the JFC should designate the component responsible for airfield operations at each base shared by Service components. The JFC will normally select the component with the preponderance of airfield operations capabilities and assets to support the airbase opening mission.

The senior airfield authority (SAA) is an individual designated by the JFC to be responsible for the control, operation, and maintenance of an airfield to include runways, associated taxiways, parking ramps, land, and facilities whose proximity affect airfield operations. In addition, it is the SAA's responsibility to define the SAA terrain boundary on a jointly inhabited installation so as to identify and establish the airfield operations activities and airfield management areas of responsibility. It is the SAA's responsibility to program for this operation area and to provide that terrain boundary identification to the BOS-I for inclusion within the overall base camp (installation) master plan. Inherent in the ability to manage these responsibilities is the task to develop a formal security plan to address security requirements for airfield operations.

COMMAND AND CONTROL ARCHITECTURES

To support taskings through both the administrative and operational chains of command, US forces have a series of C2 centers that form an integrated structure. They are capable of operations in all levels of contingencies and may represent only one Service component or more than one Service in a joint structure. These centers may have a US-only mission, or they may support multinational operations as well.

These C2 centers are sometimes described as "notional," because they can vary due to tasking by AOR-specific needs and due to the variances in the multinational force they provide. Some of these C2 centers are presented below.

The National Military Command System

The senior national civilian leadership requires a system to provide oversight and C2 of the nation's military and to execute its strategy. The National Military Command System (NMCS) is the priority component of the Global Command and Control System (GCCS) designed to support the national leadership in exercising its responsibilities. The NMCS provides the means by which the President and the SecDef can send and receive information that supports timely decisions. It also supports their communications with the combatant commanders or the commanders of other established commands. The NMCS must be capable of providing information to the senior national leadership so they can select and direct appropriate and timely responses and ensure their implementation. In addition, the NMCS supports the JCS in carrying out their responsibilities.

The NMCS includes four primary nodes (the National Military Command Center, Alternate National Military Command Center, United States Strategic Command Global Operations Center, and National Airborne Operations Center) and such other command centers as may be designated by the SecDef. Support of the NMCS is the priority function of all primary and alternate command centers.

GCCS is designed to provide an enduring command structure with survivable C2 systems. It is required and fundamental to NMCS's continuity of operations. GCCS is a comprehensive, secure, worldwide network of systems that provides the national leadership, joint staff, combatant commands, Services, defense agencies, joint task forces and functional components, and others with information processing and dissemination capabilities necessary for C2 of forces. For further detail concerning the NMCS, refer to Chairman of the Joint Chiefs of Staff Instruction (CJCSI) 6721.01A, *Global Command and Control Management Structure*, and JP 6-0, *Joint Communications System*.

Nuclear Command and Control System

The management and C2 of nuclear weapons is a joint responsibility. There is a dedicated joint C2 system that manages these weapons. The purpose of nuclear forces is to deter the use of weapons of mass destruction, particularly nuclear weapons, and to serve as a hedge against the emergence of an overwhelming conventional threat. Control of US nuclear weapons is established to preclude unauthorized or inadvertent use either by US or allied forces, foreign powers, or terrorists without degrading the operational readiness of these weapons. Command is managed via dedicated media message delivery systems standardized for joint operations. C2 must support theater and strategic employment of nuclear weapons through all phases of a conflict.

National policy requires centralized execution authority of nuclear weapons. The President is the sole authority for release of US nuclear weapons. Release and related instructions will be transmitted via the CJCS in accordance with established emergency action procedures (EAP). Air Force forces assigned or attached to USSTRATCOM execute nuclear operations under direct control of the senior national civilian leadership. For further detail concerning the nuclear C2 system, refer to JP 3-12, *Doctrine for Joint Nuclear Operations* and AFDD 2-1.5, *Nuclear Operations.*

Air Force Command and Control Centers

Air Force C2 centers must provide oversight and control for operations conducted worldwide. These centers must support both the operational and administrative chains of command. Each C2 center is unique in its mission, due to the uniqueness of the command and the mission that it serves. There is no "cookie cutter" approach to C2 node design and capabilities. These C2 centers may provide the capability to command deployed forces forward, while at the same time maintain a command presence at home station. This concept is enabled through the process of "reachback," or distributed operations.

The Air Force C2 architecture consists of strategic, operational, and tactical C2 nodes, which provide the tools by which Air Force leaders exercise C2 of forces at home station, en route, and while deployed. This doctrine document focuses mainly on the operational level of C2 with some discussion of tactical C2 operations and architecture. However, many C2 nodes span several levels of operations and cross the full range of military operations.

Reachback and Distributed Operations

Air Force C2 centers may use the concepts of reachback and distributed operations to support forces deployed or operating in place from multiple locations. Reachback is a generic term for obtaining forces, materiel, or information support from Air Force organizations not forward deployed. Communications and information systems should provide a seamless information flow of prioritized data to and from forward and rear locations. C2 of forces through the concept of reachback is normally provided from a supporting/supported relationship. This relationship gives the forward-deployed COMAFFOR the support necessary to conduct operations while maintaining a smaller deployed footprint. Effective reachback enhances the operational capability and facilitates informed and timely decision-making by the engaged COMAFFOR. The intent of reachback operations is to support forces forward, not to command operations from the rear.

Distributed operations occur when independent or interdependent nodes or locations participate in the operational planning and/or operational decision-making process to accomplish goals/missions for engaged commanders. For instance, the Joint Space Operations Center (JSpOC) can task the Global Positioning System (GPS) to provide required data to theater planners for planning of air strikes. While the relationships may vary according to the nature of the operation, the design of a distributed operation should enable a more survivable C2 network through distribution of tasks and information. In some instances, the commander may establish a formal supported/supporting relationship between distributed nodes. In other instances, distributed nodes may have a horizontal relationship. Military commanders have used distributed C2 for many years. The method and means for controlling forces have changed, but military leaders have always distributed their operations among multiple echelons. What has changed in recent years is that technology enables more participants from greater distances to create and manage complex networks.

Split operations are a type of distributed operations. The term describes those distributed operations conducted by a single C2 entity that is separated between two or more geographic locations. A single commander must have oversight of all aspects of a split C2 operation. For example, sections of the ATO may be developed from a rear area or backup operation center to reduce the deployed AOC footprint. In this case the AOC is geographically separated and is a split operation. During split operations, the COMAFFOR has the same degree of authority over geographically separated elements as he or she does over the deployed AFFOR and AOC.

Although distributed operations are similar to reachback, there is one major difference. Reachback provides ongoing combat support to the operation from the rear while a distributed operation indicates actual involvement in operational planning and/or operational decision-making. Information technology advances may further enhance distributed operations. *The goal of effective distributed operations is to support the operational commander in the field; it is not a method of command from the rear.* The concept of "reachback" allows functions to be supported by a staff at home station, to keep the manning and equipment footprint smaller at a forward location. Distributed operations, which may rely heavily on reachback support, vary by mission, circumstances, and level of conflict.

Each Air Force C2 entity will have a defined function that contributes to an overall distributed operation, whether they provide information from a fixed location at home station, or whether they are forward deployed. In a distributed C2 operation, specific roles, functions, and capabilities at each node must be fully understood and specified. Capabilities of the C2 nodes (both forward and at home station), must be thoroughly understood to effectively execute operations.

Depending on the scenario, communications capabilities, joint/combined requirements, and the political situation, C2 nodes may have to operate in the distributed operations mode. To employ distributed operations most effectively, extensive planning is required before a contingency develops. Contingency planning staffs should already have plans drawn up to accommodate a variety of C2 scenarios for deployed forces.

Air Force Component Command and Control Centers

The Air Force's C2 apparatus must be able to support worldwide distributed operations. It must integrate all aspects of air and space power; and provide for connectivity with joint and coalition operations, as required by the supported theater combatant commanders and as directed by the senior national leadership. The Air Force, whether through permanent facilities or expeditionary capability, must provide a permanent and flexible network of C2 nodes and a deployment capability that can bring global capabilities into theater focus.

The network of worldwide C2 centers is the backbone of the Air Force support of Air Force forces conducting operations worldwide and the basis for joint and coalition connectivity. Many of these nodes identified are not Air Force-exclusive, but are the primary responsibility of the Air Force as defined in Title 10, U.S.C. Although provided by the Air Force, these nodes must be able to interact with sister Service, DOD, and allied nation C2 networks. Aligned air reserve component units will provide critical augmentation to regular force structure at each node. Major commands and direct reporting agencies have specific responsibilities for each node, but the overall architecture facilitates Air Force support to the warfighter.

The C2 centers discussed below support the administrative chain of command and the operational chain. They enable the employment of Air Force forces from home station to support worldwide requirements. They also provide information to senior Air Force and national leadership.

Air Force Service Watch Cell

The Air Force Service Watch Cell (AFSWC) is the C2 organization that provides information to the Air Force operations group (AFOG) and other staffs and agencies within DOD. The mission of the AFOG is to collect, process, analyze, and communicate information enabling situational awareness of current Air Force operations worldwide. This awareness facilitates timely, responsive and effective decision-making by senior Air Force leaders and supported combatant commanders. The AFOG serves and supports the CSAF with a responsive integrated crisis action team (CAT) during national emergencies by providing operations briefings, monitoring current events, and coordinating Air Force support for joint operations.

The AFOG operates the AFSWC under the unified command center concept. It is a 24-hour operation that interfaces with the NMCC, the joint staff, sister Services, and other governmental agencies, and supports the Department of the Air Force. It also provides connectivity to the MAJCOMs and other Air Force agencies.

Major Commands, Numbered Air Forces, and Installation Control Centers

MAJCOMs and/or NAFs are authorized to operate a separate MAJCOM-dedicated command center to manage assets beyond the limits of their home station.

The mission of a MAJCOM command center is to provide commanders the global support structure to exercise C2 of assigned forces through facility, staff advice, and communication resources. This C2 center provides the continuous C2 link necessary to satisfy a commander's responsibility to control and support Air Force forces worldwide.

Each Air Force installation maintains and operates an installation control center (ICC) to provide C2 for all resident units and organizations on the installation. The ICC provides the installation commander a single, consolidated C2 center from which to monitor and execute the installation's missions, including tenant; joint; and combined missions for which the commander bears supporting responsibility. The USAF ICC provides a standardized, functional organization for all installations; facilitating the installation-level C2 across the full spectrum of operations.

The ICC is scalable and tailorable at the installation commander's direction to provide the exact C2 capability required for the unique location, mission, and operational situation of each installation. In addition to the CP function, the ICC may include provisions for a battle staff, mission planning function, operations planning and execution monitoring functions, maintenance operations, a logistics readiness center, and an emergency operations center (EOC). The ICC is linked to on-base support facilities such as the deployment control center, security forces, fire department, and hospital; as well as group and squadron unit control centers. The ICC is also linked to off-base C2 nodes including, but not limited to, the MAJCOM command center; Air Force component headquarters, AOC, and civilian EOCs, which are elements of the national incident management system.

The ICC supports the installation commander and tenant commanders, as well as transient or expeditionary forces hosted on a fixed installation, either in the continental US (CONUS) or overseas. As the installation commander for an expeditionary base, an AEW commander also uses the ICC to provide the required C2 capability. ICCs provide insight to activities required to execute the installation's mission at both fixed and expeditionary locations. The ICC consists of the following functional areas: the operations control function, the maintenance coordination function, the aerial port coordination function, reports, battle management, and incident response.

The ICC interfaces with the AOC as well as the AFFOR staff and is the key C2 center that bridges the C2 gap between operational planning and tactical execution. The ICC provides functional experts to receive, schedule, plan, and direct execution of the ATO. As required, the ICC is capable of connecting with elements of the TACS through voice and data communications. The ICC is especially effective when working with host nation representatives, tenant organizations, joint, and coalition forces.

Air Force Information Operations Center

The Air Force Information Operations Center (AFIOC), located at Lackland AFB, Texas, provides primary support to IO requirements across the full range of Air Force operations. Linked to other C2 nodes via robust communications, AFIOC can support worldwide warfighters in IO. The technical skills in C2 and computer systems security resident in AFIOC provide a solid baseline for command and control warfare.

Other Air Force C2 Centers/Nodes

Units below wing level may also have command centers, CPs, operations centers, readiness centers, or other centers for C2 of forces. These nodes are mission-specific and too varied to discuss in this level of document. They may be governed by applicable MAJCOM, NAF, or wing directives. They can be fixed or mobile, depending upon mission needs and tasking. These C2 centers may have connectivity with lateral joint, or even combined C2 centers that share the same or like mission (e.g., air defense C2 elements or contingency response elements, which are responsible for missions such as setting up an airbase).

CHAPTER THREE

AIR FORCE C2 IN THE OPERATIONAL CHAIN OF COMMAND

> *Unified direction is normally accomplished by establishing a joint force, assigning a mission or objective to the joint force commander, establishing command relationships, assigning and/or attaching appropriate forces to the joint force, and empowering the JFC with sufficient authority over the forces to accomplish the assigned mission.*
>
> **—JP 0-2, *Unified Action Armed Forces***

OPERATIONAL VERSUS ADMINISTRATIVE C2 ENVIRONMENT

For military forces to be employed, they must receive direction from the nation's senior civilian leadership. This authority flows through the operational chain of command. The chain runs from the President, through the SecDef, directly to the commanders of combatant commands for missions and forces assigned or attached to their commands. Operational forces can be employed worldwide to influence events. A robust C2 system to support these operational taskings is a necessity to support combatant commanders employing US and possibly multinational forces. This system must complement and be interoperable with the administrative C2 system that enables direction of Air Force day-to-day operations. This C2 system and the professionals who operate it support both the operational and the administrative chains of command of the military forces.

THE OPERATIONAL BRANCH

In the late 20th Century and into the 21st, joint and multinational operations have predominantly encompassed the full range of military operations; inclusive of air and space, land, sea, and special operations (SO) capabilities. Advances in capabilities among all forces and the ability to communicate over great distances have made the application of military power more dependent on the ability of the JFC to synchronize and integrate all components of the assigned forces. As a result, *joint and combined operations require an effective and efficient C2 structure to achieve success.*

Combatant commanders and leaders at all levels in the military are involved in the operational prosecution of a campaign. There are many facets of a successful campaign and many forces must come together for a campaign to be a success. The operational branch of the chain of command for the armed forces is established to provide a span of control necessary to execute operations across an entire AOR. There is a C2 system dedicated to supporting the objectives of the senior national leadership in executing military strategy. This system aids in effective C2 of joint and combined forces and in the execution of national strategy. It provides the operational control that combatant commanders require.

THE AIR AND SPACE EXPEDITIONARY TASK FORCE

The Air Force presents forces to the combatant commander as an AETF. The AETF is the organizational structure for deployed Air Force forces. The AETF presents a JFC with a task-organized, integrated package with the appropriate balance of force, sustainment, control, and force protection. The AETF presents a scalable, tailorable organization with three elements: a single commander, embodied in the COMAFFOR; appropriate C2 mechanisms; and tailored and fully supported forces. *Regardless of the size of the Air Force element, it will be organized along the lines of an AETF.*

The AETF will be tailored to the mission; this includes not only forces, but also the ability to provide C2 for those forces for the missions assigned. The AETF should draw first from in-theater resources, if available. If augmentation is needed, or if in-theater forces are not available, the AETF will draw as needed from the air and space expeditionary force (AEF) currently on rotation. These forces, whether in-theater or deployed from out of theater, should be fully supported

Within the AETF, the COMAFFOR organizes forces into expeditionary wings, groups, squadrons, flights, detachments, or elements, as necessary, to provide reasonable spans of control and command elements at appropriate levels, and to retain unit identity. Each of these units must have a C2 node that interfaces with other like elements and with higher headquarters. These C2 nodes will take advantage of the GIG to speed information up and down the chain of command.

COMAFFOR Operational Responsibilities

When forces of any Service are presented to a JFC, those forces are organized along Service lines; each of those Service components requires a clearly designated commander. **A COMAFFOR is designated whenever Air Force forces are presented to a JFC.** Depending on the scenario, the position of COMAFFOR may exist at different levels within a given theater. If a combatant commander (by definition a JFC) has Air Force forces permanently assigned to his/her command, that combatant commander should have a standing Air Force component, usually in the form of a MAJCOM or a NAF, and the MAJCOM commander is a standing COMAFFOR to that combatant commander. For example, the commander, US European Command (CDRUSEUCOM) has Air Force forces permanently assigned through US Air Forces in Europe (USAFE); the USAFE commander is thus the COMAFFOR to CDRUSEUCOM. The commander, PACAF, is similarly the standing COMAFFOR to the commander, US Pacific Command (CDRUSPACOM). This same principle applies to functional combatant commanders; for example, the COMAFFOR to the commander, US Transportation Command (CDRUSTRANSCOM) is the commander, Air Mobility Command (AMC).

If air and space assets from more than one Service are present within a joint force, the JFC normally will designate a JFACC to exploit the full capabilities of joint air and space operations. *The JFACC should be the Service component commander with the preponderance of air and space assets and the ability to plan, task, and control joint air and space operations.* If working with allies in a coalition or alliance operation, the JFACC may be designated as the CFACC. The CFACC recommends the proper employment of air and space forces from US components and the air components of other nations. The CFACC also plans, coordinates, allocates, tasks, executes, and assesses air and space operations to accomplish assigned operational missions. Because of the theater wide scope of air and space operations, the CFACC will typically maintain the same joint operations area (JOA) /theater-wide perspective as the JFC. The CFACC, as with any component commander, should not also be dual-hatted as the JFC. For more on the responsibilities of the CFACC, see JP 3-30, *Command and Control for Joint Air Operations.*

Functional component commanders exercise TACON of all forces made available for tasking. They exercise OPCON of their own forces under their Service component responsibilities. Thus, a COMAFFOR exercises OPCON of Air Force forces. When also designated as the CFACC, the COMAFFOR normally exercises TACON of any Navy, Army, Marine, Special Operations, and coalition aviation assets made available for tasking (i.e., those forces not retained for their own Service's organic operations).

When the COMAFFOR is designated the CFACC, there may be a need to establish a joint or combined staff with some or all parallel functions reflecting those of the AFFOR staff. Depending on the extent of the operation, the number of joint and coalition partners, and the physical location of the AFFOR staff (i.e., collocated with the COMAFFOR, at a reachback location, or distributed between the two), the Air Force component staff may provide the basis for the joint or combined staff. Additionally, some AFFOR staff personnel may be present in the AOC to provide the CFACC with access to Air Force component information. Augmentation within each AOC division from relevant Service components ensures adequate joint representation on the CFACC staff. At the discretion of the CFACC, officers from other Services should fill key deputy and principal staff CFACC positions. Liaison officers from other Service components and allies will provide insight and coordination between forces. When the Air Force component staff assumes CFACC staff functions, the CFACC must provide a clear definition of responsibilities and adequate resources to ensure both the Air Force component and CFACC staff functions operate effectively, yet remain functionally separate.

FUNCTIONAL AIR AND SPACE OPERATIONS ARCHITECTURES

Command and Control Arrangements for Functional Air and Space Forces

Some air and space forces are organized and employed functionally and can thus support more than one geographic combatant commander or other government agency at a time. Therefore, not all air and space forces employed in an operation will be attached forward to a geographic combatant commander. Space, air mobility, and special operations forces are organized under functional combatant commanders who normally retain control of the forces assigned to them, unless they are transferred forward by the SecDef. These forces normally operate under a support relationship to geographic commanders

C2 of Space Forces

C2 of space forces is challenging due to the fragmented nature of space operations and the interdependence between global and theater space forces. Space capabilities come from a variety of organizations, sometimes outside of the DOD with nontraditional chains of command. Also, interagency responsibilities with authority split between organizations further complicate C2 of space operations. Many space assets support joint operations in more than one geographic area. Space assets may be used to fulfill individual theater, multiple theater, or global objectives.

The C2 structure established for space forces must be robust enough to account for these various operating areas. In the administrative chain, the commander, Air Force Space Command (AFSPC/CC) exercises ADCON over Air Force space forces as the MAJCOM commander. In the operational chain, the Unified Command Plan (UCP) designates CDRUSSTRATCOM as responsible for all military space operations. CDRUSSTRATCOM has COCOM of all space forces as assigned by the SecDef. USSTRATCOM operates assigned military space forces through its joint functional component commands. *Fourteenth Air Force, Air Force Strategic Command (Space) (14AF AFSTRAT-SP) is the Air Force component to USSTRATCOM's current joint functional component command-space (JFCC-SP). The commander, JFCC Space commands and controls space forces through the JSpOC.*

Within a theater, the DIRSPACEFOR works for the COMAFFOR as the senior space advisor. The DIRSPACEFOR conducts coordination, and staffing activities to integrate space capabilities for the COMAFFOR. For more on the role of the DIRSPACEFOR see AFDD 2-2, *Space Operations*.

Space AOC/Joint Space Operations Center

The Air Force provides a space AOC that forms the core of the JSpOC. The space AOC is located at Vandenberg AFB, California. It includes personnel, facilities and equipment necessary to plan, execute and assess space operations and integrates space power on behalf of the commander, JFCC Space, into all combatant commands. The space AOC tracks assigned and attached space forces/assets and provides reachback support to organic theater space personnel. The space AOC translates CDRUSSTRATCOM's operation orders (OPORDs) and the commander, JFCC Space's guidance into space tasking orders (STO), which are a part of the overall space tasking cycle. STOs task and direct assigned and attached space forces to fulfill theater and global mission requirements in support of national objectives. The STO production cycle is based on the standard 72-hour ATO cycle. The STO cycle is flexible to synchronize with the theater battle rhythm. The primary functions of the space AOC are to:

✪ Serve as the JFCC Space's point of contact for space operations issues.

✪ Advise USSTRATCOM on space strategy and campaign plans.

✪ Task and direct assigned and attached space forces via the STO.

✪ Conduct planning, tasking, integration, command, control, and operational execution for global space operations.

✪ Maintain a COP for space capabilities and ensure it is available to combatant commanders for situational awareness.

Space AOC Organization

The space AOC is a functional AOC composed of four divisions: strategy, combat plans, combat operations and ISR. There are also specialty teams, liaisons from other agencies and sister Service and allied officers to enable the space AOC to fulfill its responsibilities as the JSpOC. Collectively, they accomplish the main processes of strategy development, planning, tasking, collection management, and intelligence analysis/production. The space AOC serves as the Air Force focal point for coordination and reachback support for regional space operations requirements. For more information, see AFDD 2-2, *Space Operations,* and AFOTTP 2-3.4, *Space Air and Space Operations Center*.

C2 of Cyberspace Forces

C2 of cyberspace forces is evolving. The Air Force views cyberspace as a domain that uses the electromagnetic spectrum as its maneuver space to conduct global operations. Comprehending cyberspace as a domain allows an understanding of its expansive global nature and how best to design organizations and capabilities to best exploit it. The CSAF designated Eighth Air Force (8 AF) as the operational command for cyberspace. Eighth Air Force's mission will be to integrate the Air Force's global kinetic and non-kinetic strike capability in support of the combatant commander through the full range of military operations.

C2 of Cyberspace Forces

Doctrine for cyberspace operations (including its C2) is under development. As doctrine for cyberspace operations is developed, it will be incorporated into Air Force doctrine documents as they are revised. Key points in this ongoing process are discussed below.

✪ The new Air Force mission statement, "…deliver sovereign options for the defense of the United States of America and its global interests – to fly and fight in air, space and cyberspace" explicitly recognizes cyberspace's growing importance to the nation's defense.

✪ The current JCS-endorsed working definition of cyberspace identifies it as a new domain and makes it more than simply a subset of the information environment or a subset of information operations.

✪ The CSAF designated 8 AF as the operational command for cyberspace. Eighth Air Force's mission will be to integrate the Air Force's global kinetic and non-kinetic strike capability in support of the combatant commander through the full range of military operations.

✪ Effectively employing forces in this new domain may require changes in the way we present forces to the joint fight. Defining how we command and control these assets will be an important first step

✪ CSAF issued a "Go Do" letter directing 8 AF to stand up the Air Force's Cyber Command, including an AOC, to be interoperable with other Air Force AOCs.

—Various Sources

Air Force Network Operations Center

To ensure the availability of the GIG and its continuous protection, the AFNETOPS/CC, via the AFNETOPS center, provides oversight of the forces responsible for building, operating, and defending the Air Force portion of the GIG. The AFNETOPS center is located at 8 AF headquarters, Barksdale AFB, Louisiana.

The Air Force GIG C2 system enables the AFNETOPS/CC to provide support to the commander, JTF-Global Network Operations (GNO), and the designated COMAFFOR for each combatant commander. It provides these commanders the capability to plan and conduct global NETOPS and to ensure GIG availability and security in support of joint and combined operations. The AFNETOPS center provides Air Force staff and execution functions for the Air Force component that supports JTF-GNO. The CDRUSSTRATCOM provides guidance to 8 AF/CC, who develops and executes the Air Force component portion of the USSTRATCOM NETOPS campaign plan.

C2 of Air Mobility Forces

Air mobility forces are divided into intertheater forces and intratheater forces, each comprising separate yet mutually supporting C2 systems, with differing C2 arrangements for each mission. *Intertheater* air mobility involves forces operating between the CONUS and a geographic combatant command's AOR or between two geographic combatant commands' AORs. These operations require close coordination between AMC and the theater air components. Intertheater air mobility operations are generally global in scope and serve the CONUS-to-theater air transportation and force projection needs of the geographic combatant commander. *Intratheater* operations cover two types of operations, those of a single geographic combatant commander during peacetime or when a JOA has not been established, and those operations inside a JOA when a joint task force has been established. In both of these situations operations are normally conducted using forces assigned, attached, or made available for tasking to the JFC.

For air mobility forces performing primarily intertheater operations the preferred command relationship between global/functional and regional/geographic organizations is support. Within a theater, this support relationship is normally facilitated by the designated DIRMOBFOR-AIR attached to the AETF. When forces are attached to a theater, JP 0-2 states, "The combatant commander normally exercises OPCON over forces attached." See AFDD 2 for a detailed discussion of recommended command relationships for non-assigned forces.

CDRUSTRANSCOM exercises COCOM over CONUS-based active duty air mobility forces, as well as some overseas deployed expeditionary mobility task force (EMTF) air mobility support forces even though they are assigned to USTRANSCOM. CDRUSTRANSCOM normally will delegate OPCON of these forces to the Air Force component commander (who is the commander, AMC), who further delegates the day-to-day execution authority to the commander, 18th Air Force (18 AF).

When USTRANSCOM air mobility forces are deployed for extended durations in supporting operations, they are normally organized as expeditionary units. Because these forces are located within geographic theater boundaries, an ADCON relationship is normally established with the Air Force host command to ensure that support requirements are met. Command-to-command agreements are the best method for detailing these arrangements.

18 AF (AFTRANS) 618th Tanker Airlift Control Center

For global operations, the 18 AF/CC executes centralized control of AMC-assigned or attached forces through the 18 AF tanker airlift control center (618 TACC). The 18 AF/CC responds to air mobility requirements handed down from

USTRANSCOM. Located at Scott AFB, Illinois, the 618 TACC is AMC's hub for planning, scheduling, tasking, and executing assigned air mobility forces around the world. The 618 TACC is designated as a functional AOC. The 18 AF/TACC is dedicated to providing quality service to a wide range of mobility customers. Its number one mission is to provide quality mobility support to the President and combatant commanders. Because of air mobility's global responsibility, multiple competing common users, and the necessity to prioritize and apportion limited resources, centralized control of air mobility is crucial. The 618 TACC directs intertheater mobility forces through its air mobility wings and EMTFs.

> *Named 'Operation Vittles,' the airlift forced AACS [Airways and Air Communication Service] personnel to improvise new methods of air traffic control to handle the volume of traffic needed to bring the minimum 4,500 tons of coal and food into Berlin daily... The area control operators kept in touch with the aircraft until they turned them over to the ground-controlled approach radar operators who talked them down to a safe landing. Airplanes that missed their first landing approach were dispatched back to their home base unless they could be later vectored back into the landing pattern. Flight plans, position reports, and clearance phraseology were streamlined to limit the length of radio transmissions and accelerate operations. Ground-controlled approach radar was the keystone upon which the airlift system was built.*
>
> **—Thomas S. Snyder, ed.,** ***History of Air Force Communications Command***

The 618 TACC plans and executes all USTRANSCOM-owned tanker, airlift, and support missions and monitors commercial contract airlift missions. It performs detailed pre-mission planning and provides that information to the air mobility units, the airlift and tanker crews, and operating locations for mission execution. During execution, the 18 AF/CC exercises OPCON over USTRANSCOM-owned Air Force crews and aircraft until return to home station. Within a regional JTF, the DIRMOBFOR-AIR provides the links between the regional air component's air mobility operations and the TACC's intertheater air mobility operations.

618 TACC Organization

The 618 TACC consists of eight divisions led by a director of operations who provides immediate oversight and decision-making in the day-to-day missions of AMC, and serves as the command's representative to the joint staff, AFSWC, NMCC, USTRANSCOM, DOD, and other agencies. The divisions are: mobility management, command and control, current operations, global readiness, global channel operations, operations management, intelligence, and the 15th Operational Weather Squadron. There are also Air Force Reserve and Air National Guard advisors who provide advice and guidance on air reserve components (ARC) matters. For a more detailed description, see AFDD 2-6, *Air Mobility Operations*.

C2 of Special Operations

SO are conducted in hostile, denied, or politically sensitive environments to achieve military, diplomatic, informational, and/or economic objectives. Special operations employ military capabilities for which there are no broad conventional force requirements. These operations often require covert or low-visibility capabilities. SO are applicable across the range of military operations. They can be conducted independently or in conjunction with operations of conventional forces or other government agencies and may include operations by, with, or through indigenous or surrogate forces.

SOF may be assigned to either US Special Operations Command (USSOCOM) or a geographic combatant command. OPCON of SOF assigned to a geographic combatant command is exercised by the commander of the theater special operations command (TSOC). OPCON of SOF attached to a geographic combatant command is normally exercised by the commander of the TSOC or other JFC (e.g., commander, joint special operations task force [JSOTF], etc.).

SOF are most effective when SO are fully integrated into the overall campaign plan (war or stability operations). Successful execution of SO requires clear, responsive C2 by an appropriate SOF C2 element. The limited window of opportunity normally associated with the majority of SOF missions, as well as the sensitive nature of many of these missions, requires a C2 structure that is, above all, responsive to the needs of the operational unit. SOF C2 may be tailored for a specific mission or operation. Liaison among all components of the joint force and SOF, wherever assigned, is vital for effective employment of SOF as well as the prevention of fratricide.

A JSOTF is a JTF composed of SO units from more than one Service formed to carry out a specific SO or prosecute SO in support of a theater campaign or other operations. When the JSOTF is combined with conventional forces as part of a larger joint force, it will often be designated as a functional component—Joint Force Special Operation Component. A JSOTF may have conventional non-special operations units assigned or attached to support the conduct of specific missions, or such forces may be tasked to provide support. A JSOTF, like any JTF, is normally established by a JFC (e.g., a combatant commander, a subordinate unified commander such as a TSOC commander, or a JTF commander). For example, a geographic combatant commander could establish a JTF to conduct operations in a specific region of the theater. Either the geographic combatant commander or the JTF commander could then establish a JSOTF, subordinate to that JTF, to plan and execute SO. Likewise, a TSOC commander could establish a JSOTF to focus on a specific mission or region assigned by the geographic combatant commander. A JSOTF may also be established as a joint organization and deployed as an entity from outside the theater.

Special Operations Forces Liaison Elements

SOF commanders have available specific elements that facilitate C2, coordination, and liaison. They include the special operations C2 element (SOCCE) to provide C2 and coordinate SOF activities with conventional forces; the special operations liaison element (SOLE) to provide liaison to the CFACC or appropriate Service component air C2 facility; and SOF liaison officers (LNOs) placed in a variety of locations as necessary to coordinate, synchronize, and deconflict SO within the operational area. All of these and other SOF C2 elements significantly improve the flow of information, facilitate concurrent planning, and enhance overall mission accomplishment of the joint force.

Air Force Special Operations C2

The Air Force special operations component (not to be confused with the Air Force Special Operations Command [AFSOC], the Air Force component of USSOCOM) is the Air Force component of a joint SO force. It is normally composed of a special operations wing, special operations group, or special tactics group. When subordinate Air Force SOF units deploy to forward operations bases (FOBs) or advanced operations bases (AOBs), the AFSOC commander may establish one or more provisional units. The Air Force special operations detachment (AFSOD) is a squadron-size Air Force Special Operations Forces (AFSOF) unit that could be a composite organization composed of different Air Force assets. The detachment normally is subordinate to a theater Air Force special operations component, JSOTF, joint special operations air component commander (JSOACC), or JTF depending upon the size and duration of the operation. The Air Force special operations element (AFSOE) contains selected AFSOF units and is normally subordinate to a theater Air Force special operations component or AFSOD, depending upon the size and duration of the operation.

C2 of Regional Air Force Forces

Air Force Component Headquarters

The Air Force is establishing Air Force component headquarters capable of providing the unified combatant commander and his designated JFCs the full spectrum of air, space, and cyberspace capabilities. The Air Force must be able to employ forces anywhere in the world, in support of national security objectives. To achieve this goal, the designated COMAFFOR must be ready to quickly establish the C2 functions necessary to control air, space, and cyberspace operations. The COMAFFOR must also be prepared to serve as the CFACC or as the JTF commander if requested (CFACC and JTF/CC positions should not normally be dual-hatted).

The construct establishes component organizations, some of which will be regionally focused and some which will be globally focused. Each will have an AFFOR staff and an appropriately tailored AOC. The Air Force component headquarters will vary in size, depending on factors such as geographic location, responsibilities, and missions assigned. These Air Force component headquarters are intended to be the Airman's single voice to the JFC. This reorganization is designed to enhance combat capability, integrate combat staffs with AOCs, and provide the JFC an air and space-focused warfighting structure supported by state-of-the-art warfighting C2.

All of these headquarters will be integrated into a robust communications network. This will facilitate collaborative planning and the rapid transfer of AOC functions between headquarters in the event an AOC is taken down.

Air and Space Operations Center

The AOC is the operational-level warfighting command center for air and space forces. As a component organization of the Air Force, the AOC is the air and space operations planning and execution focal point for the COMAFFOR. In most large scale operations the Air Force will provide the preponderance of air assets and possess the necessary capabilities to exercise C2 over all theater air operations. Accordingly, the Air Force component commander will normally be designated the CFACC. The AOC provides the air and space component commander the capability to plan, execute, and assess air and space operations. The AOC is often referred to as a CAOC in Air Force doctrine documents. However, this document discusses the variations in the Air Force AOC weapon system. To simplify discussion, the term "AOC" will be used unless there is need for a specific reference to a CAOC vice an AOC. Along with the CFACC's senior staff, the AOC's various divisions and teams are responsible for planning, executing, and assessing air and space operations. Through the AOC, the CFACC directs tactical actions to produce desired operational and strategic effects in support of the JFC's campaign. The fundamental principle of this system is centralized planning and control through the AOC, with decentralized execution by subordinate/tasked organizations and elements. For a more detailed examination of the AOC, see AFOTTP 2-3.2, *Air and Space Operations Center*.

The AOC is nominally designed and organized to conduct intense air operations consistent with major operations and campaigns. However, it can be configured to conduct operations across the range of military operations. Each AOC crew is uniquely trained to the local environment, resource availability, operational demands, and command relationships of the military and civilian hierarchy in its AOR.

The AOC is an Air Force weapon system, known as the Falconer. There are three types of AOCs: the Falconer, the tailored Falconer, and the functional Falconer AOC. Falconer AOCs are assigned to specific geographic combatant commanders (GCCs), and can be fixed, deployable, or a combination of both of these options. A tailored Falconer is a variant adapted for specific or unique missions, such as 1 AF's AOC, which supports the homeland security mission. Functional AOCs support global functional requirements. AMC has a functional AOC, the 618 TACC. In addition, the Space AOC is a functional AOC, capable of C2 over the broad range of assigned USSTRATCOM space missions. Functional AOCs correspond as much as possible to Falconer AOCs.

AOC Organization and Employment

The Falconer AOC is notionally organized under an AOC commander (AOC/CC), with five divisions (strategy; combat plans; combat operations; intelligence, surveillance, and reconnaissance; and air mobility), and multiple support/specialty teams. Each specialty/support team is a horizontally cross-cutting capability integrated into the five divisions.   Figure 3.1 depicts a notional AOC organization. The AOC/CC acts as the JAOC Director in a JAOC/CAOC, having no command authority over augmentees from other Service components or allied/coalition personnel.

The Falconer is usually employed as the senior element of the TACS and provides centralized planning, direction, control, and coordination of air and space operations. The AOC may be employed in a scenario that does not require the full TACS for mission execution, such as a stability operation (or in space or mobility operations, which use tailored or functional Falconers). Some scenarios, such as major operations and campaigns, usually require the AOC to employ with a full TACS. The AOC may be fixed or mobile, depending upon the level of contingency, theater or scenario requirements, and political and diplomatic situations. The AOC is configured to meet its functional or regional mission and AOC crews train to meet the unique requirements for various scenarios in the appropriate AOR or functional scenario.

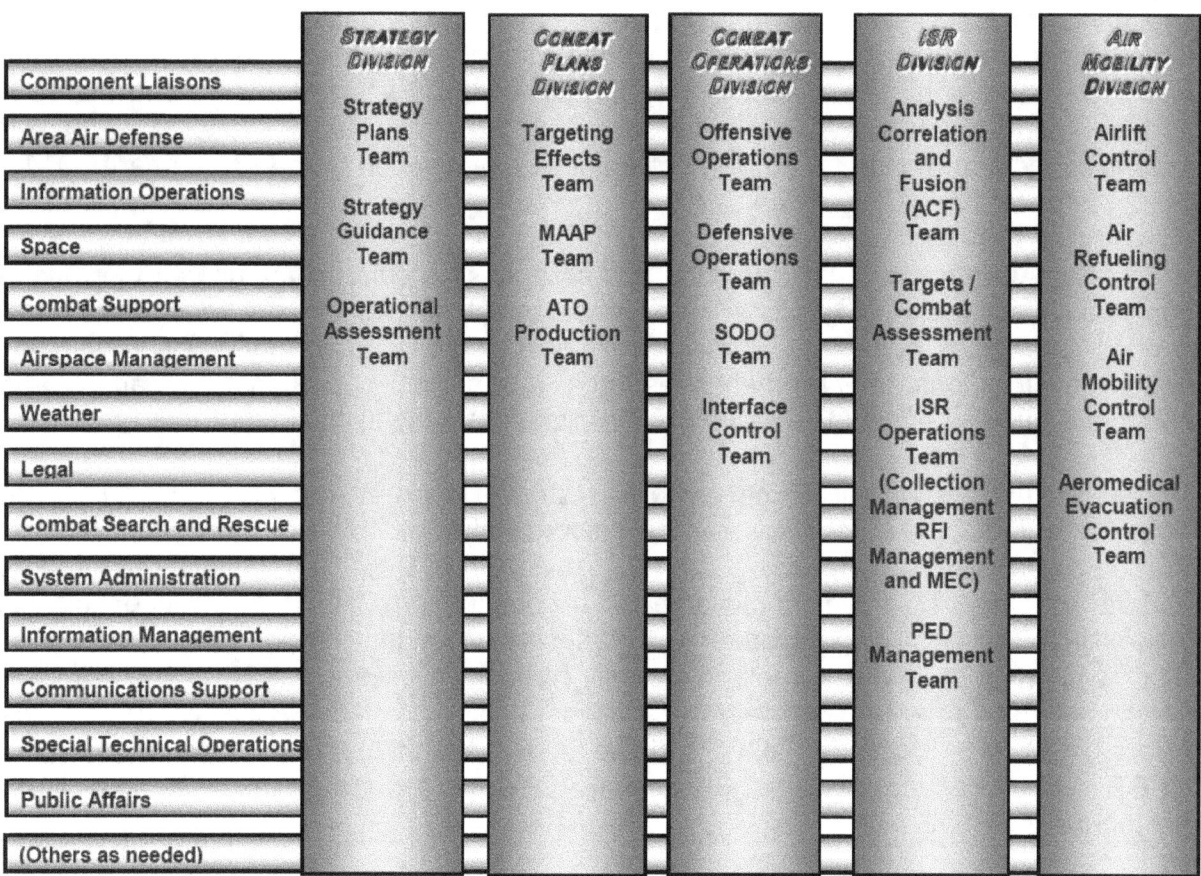

Figure 3.1. Basic Structure of a Notional AOC.

Component Liaisons, Coalition and Allied Liaisons, Coordination Elements, and Specialty/Support Functions

The AOC also has component liaisons, coordination elements, and specialty teams that assist the COMAFFOR and/or CFACC in executing the air and space portions of the campaign. Component liaisons are provided by each Service or functional component commander involved in the operation of the AOC to articulate component requirements. The special operations component commander provides a SOLE to coordinate, integrate, and synchronize SOF operations, strategy, and plans with conventional air. The other Services have a liaison presence in the AOC. The battlefield coordination detachment (BCD) represents the Army, while the naval and amphibious liaison element (NALE) articulates Navy and Marine interests, unless a separate Marine liaison officer (MARLO) is designated.

For large operations, the CFACC may establish one or more air component coordination elements (ACCEs) with the JFC's or a component commander's headquarters to better integrate air and space operations with surface operations, and with the JTF headquarters to better integrate air and space operations within the overall joint force. When established, these elements act as the CFACC's primary representatives to the respective commanders and facilitate interaction between the respective staffs. The ACCE also communicates the component commander's decisions and interests to the CFACC. However, the ACCE should not replace, replicate, or circumvent normal request mechanisms already in place in the component/JTF staffs. The ACCE is a liaison function, not a C2 node. It normally has no authority to direct or execute operations. The make-up of the ACCE is dependent on the scope of the operation and the size of the staff they will liaise with. The ACCE should be tailored with the expertise necessary to perform effectively. Element expertise may include plans, operations, intelligence, airspace management, logistics, space, and air mobility, as needed.

LNOs representing coalition and/or allied forces may improve AOC situational awareness regarding the disposition of friendly forces and their inclusion in coalition operations. They are also essential for unity of effort for coalition air defense operations and airspace deconfliction. The AOC commander should anticipate the need for LNOs during both the planning and execution phases of an operation. For more information concerning coalition and allied liaison officers see JP 3-0.

The regional air movement control center (RAMCC) is a specialty team that provides the CFACC with a centralized function to deconflict both military and civilian air traffic in a particular airspace control area. The goal of the RAMCC is to provide a safe and efficient operating environment through managing the complex interaction of military and civil aircraft attempting to access or transit the airspace control area. The RAMCC may include liaison officers from the coalition and neutral nations and will have interface with nongovernmental organizations and civil or commercial users of the airspace. For related discussion, see AFDD 2-1.7, *Airspace Control in the Combat Zone*.

The Airborne Command Element (ACE) is an optional element composed of a single officer or team of mission experts who fly on board airborne C2 platforms and function as the CFACC's representative. When required, the ACE conducts the air battle in accordance with the latest command guidance.

The Theater Air Control System

The Air Force TACS reflects the air and space power tenet of centralized control and decentralized execution. The TACS provides the COMAFFOR with the means to achieve this tenet. The AOC is the senior element of the TACS. The TACS can be tailored to support contingencies ranging from the smallest stability operation to full-scale combat operations. TACS elements may be employed in garrison, deployed for contingencies or deployed to augment theater-specific systems. The TACS is divided into ground and airborne elements. When the TACS is combined with other components' C2 elements, such as the Army air-ground system, the Navy tactical air control system, and the Marine Corps air command and control system, they become the theater air-ground system (TAGS), to execute operations for the CFACC. For a more detailed examination of each element of the TACS, see AFDD 2-1.7, *Airspace Control in the Combat Zone* and AFTTP 3-1, Vol. 26, *Theater Air Control System.* Figure 3.2 presents a notional depiction of the TACS, including connectivity among elements.

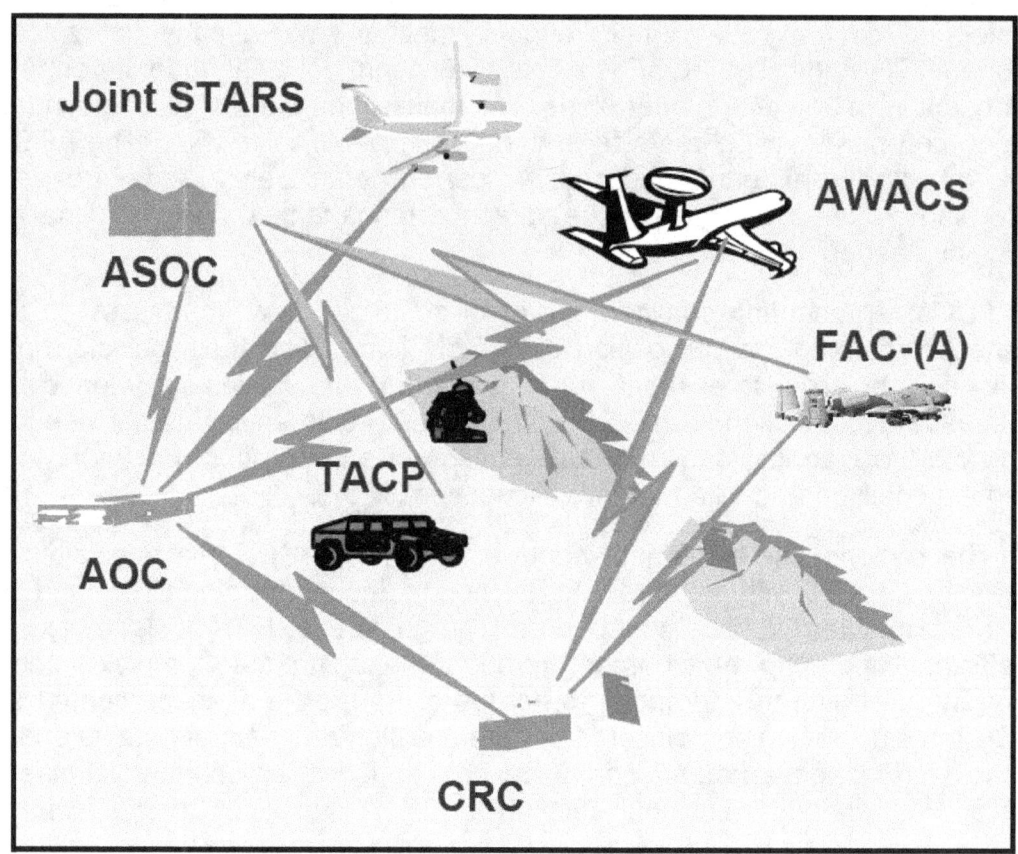

Figure 3.2. Notional Theater Air Control System.

Ground Theater Air Control System Elements

Ground theater air control system (GTACS) elements include the control and reporting centers (CRC), the ASOC, and the TACP. The CRC is subordinate to the AOC and may be designated as the primary theater command, control, and air surveillance facility within the theater, or may share that responsibility with other TACS elements such as AWACS. Responsibility as the region/sector air defense commander is also normally decentralized to the CRC, which acts as the primary integration point for air defense artillery (ADA) fire control. The CRC may deploy mobile radars and associated communications equipment to expand radar coverage and communications range within its assigned operating area. These remote radars are capable of providing early warning, surveillance, weapons control, and identification functions. The ASOC, which reports to the AOC, receives, coordinates, and processes requests for immediate air support from subordinate TACPs, which are transmitted through the joint air request net (JARN). ASOCs commit allocated sorties to satisfy requests for immediate air support and integrate those missions with the supported units' fires and maneuver. An ASOC is normally tasked to support an Army unit but can also support units from other organizations (e.g., special operations, coalition forces). It may also augment other missions requiring C2 of air assets (e.g., humanitarian efforts). TACPs are aligned with Army maneuver elements, battalion through corps level. They are primarily responsible for decentralized execution of CAS operations. TACPs request, coordinate, and control CAS and theater airlift missions as required. For more information on TACPs and ASOCs, see AFDD 2-1.3, *Counterland*.

Airborne Elements of the Theater Air Control System

Airborne elements of the theater air control system (AETACS) elements include the AWACS, the joint surveillance target attack radar system (JSTARS), and the forward air controller (airborne) (FAC [A]). AWACS is subordinate to the AOC and conducts air surveillance and supports strategic attack, counterair, counterland, air refueling operations, and other air and space power functions/missions as directed. JSTARS provides dedicated support to ground commanders and attack support functions to friendly offensive air elements. The FAC(A) is an airborne extension of the TACP and has the authority to direct aircraft delivering ordnance to a specific target cleared by the ground commander. The FAC(A) provides additional flexibility in the operational environment by enabling rapid coordination and execution of air operations. It also enhances the TACS'

Problems coordinating close air support operations over long distances during Operation ANACONDA highlighted the need for an airborne C2 and communications relay platform in the role formerly occupied by the Airborne Command and Control Center. In the future, portions of this mission will be shared by AWACS, Joint STARS, and unmanned aircraft.

situational awareness by disseminating information on the flow of aircraft on target.

Air Force C2 in Homeland Operations

The DOD contributes to homeland security (HS) through homeland defense (HD), emergency preparedness (EP), and defense support of civil authorities (DSCA). The *National Strategy for Homeland Security* provides a federal framework for a concerted national effort to prevent terrorist attacks within the United States, reduce America's vulnerability to terrorism, as well as minimize the damage and recover from attacks that do occur. The DOD uses "homeland security" as an umbrella term to include homeland defense, emergency preparedness, and defense support of civil authorities (whether combating terrorism or supporting domestic incident management after an earthquake or other natural disaster). For the Air Force, homeland operations are the means by which its support to homeland security is accomplished.

The commander, US Northern Command (CDRUSNORTHCOM) and CDRUSPACOM are the supported JFCs for homeland operations. For homeland defense in the NORTHCOM area of responsibility, less the Alaska JOA, the commander, First Air Force (Air Forces Northern) (1 AF [AFNORTH]/CC) has been designated as the COMAFFOR, and acts as a JFACC with OPCON of air forces for homeland operations. For the Alaska JOA, the commander, Alaska North American Aerospace Defense (NORAD) Region (CDRANR) (11th Air Force) acts as a JFACC with OPCON of homeland defense air forces. Both JFACCs supporting USNORTHCOM provide assets in direct support of JTF requirements.

If National Guard assets are involved in these operations they may be operating under gubernatorial authority in Title 32 or state active duty status, or under federal authority in Title 10 status. It is imperative the command arrangements and relationships for National Guard operations mesh with those set up by CDRUSNORTHCOM and CDRUSPACOM to ensure deconfliction of efforts and effective allocation of resources to prevent duplication.

Air National Guard assets have been the primary Air Force forces involved in homeland defense operations. While ANG personnel routinely operate under gubernatorial authority in Title 32 status, procedures have been established so that, upon declaration of an air sovereignty event, the ANG pilot immediately assumes Title 10 (federal operations) status. This command arrangement/relationship for Air National Guard operations in homeland defense dovetails with the CDRUSNORTHCOM/commander in chief, NORAD (CINCNORAD) and CDRUSPACOM/ CINCNORAD requirements for effective allocation of air defense resources.

Air Force C2 in Disaster Relief and Other Operations

DSCA, often referred to as civil support, is DOD support provided during and in the aftermath of domestic emergencies—such as terrorist attacks or major disasters—and for designated law enforcement and other activities. It includes military assistance for civil law enforcement operations in very limited circumstances. However, National

Guard forces operating in state status (in state active duty and under Title 32, U.S.C.) can directly assist civil law enforcement operations. DSCA missions include, but are not limited to, supporting the Department of Justice in preventing or defeating terrorist attacks; response to chemical, biological, radiological, or nuclear incidents; response to natural disasters such as earthquakes, floods, and fires; support to civilian law enforcement agencies, including counter-drug activities; and response to civil disturbances or insurrection. In all these missions, various federal, state, or local civilian agencies are primarily responsible for the management of the particular incident. Under the homeland operations concept, the Air Force's involvement is supportive and dependent on a request to the DOD from the designated lead agency. Traditionally, DSCA operations were either considered crisis or consequence management. Crisis management activities were handled by the Federal Bureau of Investigations and consequence management by the Federal Emergency Management Agency. That distinction is now replaced with domestic incident management, a full-spectrum perspective that sees each event as a single incident requiring an integrated response.

For most homeland security scenarios, Air Force forces should be presented as an AETF under the OPCON of a COMAFFOR, just as in any other theater. For homeland operations in the NORTHCOM AOR, 1 AF at Tyndall AFB, Florida, normally fulfills the role of Air Force component to USNORTHCOM, the supported combatant command. The commander, 1AF, is also the CFACC within the NORAD chain for the CONUS NORAD region. The command relationships between a JFC and a COMAFFOR in a homeland context should be as previously described for any other region—although legal and interagency considerations may have a significant impact. *The CONUS is not a special case regarding C2 or organization of air and space forces.* Single-Service task forces may also be established in homeland operations. See AFDD 2, *Organization and Employment*, and AFDD 2-10, *Homeland Operations*, for more information on homeland operations.

Additionally, Civil Air Patrol (CAP) as an auxiliary of the Air Force can be used to perform Air Force assigned missions. These non-combatant missions encompass homeland operations, search and rescue, disaster relief and support to law enforcement authorities. See AFI 10-2701, *Organization and Function of the Civil Air Patrol,* for more information.

Air Force C2 in Continental US Air Defense Operations

The commander, 1AF, in his role as the CONUS NORAD region (CONR) commander, provides CDRNORAD/commander, US Element NORAD with surveillance and control of the airspace of the United States and appropriate response against air attack. The CONUS region commander is operationally responsible for centralized command of the CONUS region air defense activities. Decentralized control may be executed by the three air defense sectors (ADS). They are responsible for the tactical execution of air sovereignty and defense through detection, identification, and required tactical response. The ADS integrates fighters, tankers, air defense artillery assets, surface radars, and other US agencies' aircraft for air defense missions. During homeland defense operations, ground-based and airborne radar elements of the TACS support air operations primarily by providing low-level gap filler coverage and relaying

C2 guidance in the event fighters are below the ADS' radar or radio coverage. For more on CONUS air defense operations, see AFTTP(I) 3-2.50, *Air Defense of the United States* (Classified).

CHAPTER FOUR

COMMAND AND CONTROL PROCESSES

> " . . . [A] good plan violently executed now is better than a perfect plan next week."
>
> —Gen. George S. Patton, Jr.

C2 OF AIR FORCE FUNCTIONS

The COMAFFOR's mission is to command, control, and execute air and space capabilities across the full range of military operations. He must be provided a means to accomplish this task. JP 1-02 states, "C2 functions for the joint and Service force are performed through an arrangement of personnel, equipment, communications, facilities, and procedures employed by a commander in planning, directing, coordinating, and controlling forces and operations in the accomplishment of the mission." All Air Force functions require C2 for effective employment. The processes and functions described below are required for a commander to effectively plan and execute a military operation. These functions, combined with a C2 system to monitor the progress of the operation and provide feedback, will aid in the successful prosecution of the military operation. The C2 functions as discussed in JP 1-02 are discussed below.

Effective C2 decisions use a dynamic process that starts when data are received from various sources and are analyzed to form information. This information is then used as the basis for making decisions. Once the appropriate decisions are made, the commander formulates guidance and communicates it to subordinates for execution. Often, these C2 decision processes are continuous and proactive in the sense that many decisions are planned for in advance and are not normally done in a reactive manner. The Air Force uses principles of EBAO in this process to ensure there is a coherent plan that logically supports and ties all objectives and the end state together. The C2 decision process occurs at all levels of command with the key objective of making or delegating rational and timely decisions.

PLANNING

Plans are an important way for the JFC to communicate intent to subordinates and unify the efforts of the joint force. Joint force operational planning links the tactical employment of forces to campaign and strategic objectives through the achievement of operational goals. JP 5-0, *Joint Operations Planning*, gives a full description of the joint planning process. The focus of JFC planning is on operational art and design.

Operational art is the thought process commanders use to visualize how best to efficiently and effectively employ military capabilities to accomplish their mission. Operational design is the practical extension of operational art. Together they synthesize the intuition and creativity of the commander with the analytical and logical process of design The JFC requires a C2 structure that enables effective planning, execution, and assessment for his/her mission to be successful.

Planning is one process essential to effectively commanding and controlling military operations. Military operations must be extensively planned and then monitored, assessed, and adapted to shape the operational environment to create the desired effects that will ensure success. Planning is the process of examining the environment, relating objectives with resources, and deciding on a COA. Commanders make planning decisions through a rational analysis of costs, evaluation of benefits, and an acceptance of residual risks approach. The key C2 component of these planning activities is the commander's estimate process.

JP 1-02 defines the commander's estimate of a situation as "a logical process of reasoning by which a commander considers all the circumstances affecting the military situation and arrives at a decision as to a COA to be taken to accomplish the mission." The air component assists in the development of the JFC's estimate, specifically: assessing the mission, developing COAs that are responsive to the situation, analyzing adversary COAs (defend, reinforce, attack, withdraw, escalate, and delay), comparing friendly COAs, and selecting a COA, or possibly multiple COAs.

As detailed in AFDD 2, the Air Force's estimate process integrates air and space power into COAs that are presented to the JFC for a decision. The estimate process is the primary way for Airmen to influence the JFC's COA decision process. The time relationship between the JFC's and the Air Force component's estimate processes is critical. Both processes are interrelated and should be accomplished simultaneously. A desired goal is to have one staff, one process, and one product.

A JFC may also need to synthesize COAs from those recommended by subordinates in order to satisfy the criteria of suitability, feasibility, acceptability, variety, and completeness. The inputs of Airmen are critical in this synthesis process. Air and space power requires early consideration when integrating air and space missions into a campaign plan. Planning based solely upon deconfliction and synchronization, either geographically or temporally, denies air and space power its flexibility. Planning should focus on integrating air and space power into operations that will achieve specific objectives and effects.

The Air Force employs the joint air estimate process (JAEP), the air, space, and cyberspace component's extension of the joint operations planning process (JOPP). It is a six-phase process that culminates with the production of the JAOP. For more on the joint air estimate process, see JP 3-30, *Command and Control for Joint Air Operations*. The JAEP may be employed during contingency planning, producing joint air operations plans supporting operation plans or operation plans in concept format, or crisis action planning (CAP) in concert with other theater operations planning. While the phases are presented in sequential order, work on them can be either concurrent or sequential. Nevertheless, the phases are integrated and the products of each phase are checked and verified for coherence. The phases are mission analysis, situation and COA development, COA analysis, COA comparison, COA selection, COA assessment, and JAOP development.

Once the JFC decides on a COA, joint and Service component commanders develop their plans to support the JFC's overall objectives. The CFACC produces the detailed plan to achieve assigned objectives for air and space forces. The JAOP is the output of this process and forms the basis for day-to-day tactical operations. Another important JFC decision is the apportionment of air and space power to accomplish the JAOP. In turn, the CFACC allocates JFC-apportioned air power to satisfy joint objectives.

There are many notional decision-making models available for use such as the OODA loop; Lawson's model (sense, process, compare, decide, and act); and the generic monitor, assess, plan, execute (MAPE) model, which uses the effects-based construct. The Air Force C2 capabilities must be able to monitor, assess, plan, and execute the Air Force's air, space, and information missions to be effective. The following definitions of planning and execution capabilities and processes bring into focus the continuum of action required to link operational capabilities to achieve desired effects. The four sub-capabilities that make up this capability are monitoring, assessing, planning, and executing.

- ✪ **Monitoring** involves the processes of collecting, storing, maintaining, and tracking data.

- ✪ **Assessing** results is the ability to determine the nature and impact of conditions and events on force capabilities and commander's intent. It involves the processes of analyzing and evaluating information collected in the monitoring function, aided by modeling and simulation, to describe situational awareness and alternative solutions.

- ✪ **Planning** is how we develop courses of action based on information collected in the monitoring function. This information is analyzed in the assess function to support the operational objectives; develop, evaluate, and select courses of action; generate force lists (capabilities) and force movement requirements; and detail the timing of sequential actions. Planning is essentially a description and prioritization of how to achieve stated mission goals.

- ✪ **Executing** is the overall dissemination and action of the plan, synchronization of forces, and adjustment of operations in response to assessment to ensure successful mission accomplishment.

THE AIR FORCE COMPONENT PLANNING PROCESS

Planning for Deployment, Employment, Sustainment, and Redeployment of Air Force Forces

The US Armed Forces provide the military dimension of national power projection. Power projection is defined in the joint lexicon as the ability of a nation to apply all or some of its elements of national power—diplomatic, economic, informational, or military—to rapidly and effectively deploy and sustain forces in and from multiple dispersed locations to respond to crises, to contribute to deterrence, and to enhance regional stability. Military forces can be used as part of our national security strategy for force projection. The joint definition of force projection is: "The ability to project the military element of national power from the CONUS or another theater, in response to requirements for military operations. Force projection operations extend from mobilization and deployment of forces to redeployment to CONUS or home theater." Allied with this concept is the joint concept of focused logistics, which defines the support and control activities to deliver warfighting capability. This capability is a core aspect of deployment, redeployment, and sustainment of military forces. C2 professionals must employ force projection and focused logistics to plan for deployment, employment, sustainment, and redeployment of C2 forces, depending on the nature of the tasked mission.

One aspect of planning for the employment of forces is preparing the operational environment. Each operation, each theater, and each command arrangement will bring differing requirements for the employment of C2 systems. Planning and preparation in advance of a tasking are essential to a successful operation. Planning must also be performed for post-hostilities scenarios, such as nation-building or redeployment of forces. Operations do not cease simply because combat operations have terminated.

Preparing the operational environment is defined as assessing, developing, and posturing for the employment of forces in an operational area. This environment includes the factors and conditions that must be understood to successfully apply combat power, protect the force, and complete the mission. Actions include but are not limited to:

✪ Knowing the operational environment, factors, and conditions.

✪ Performing intelligence gathering and disseminating intelligence.

✪ Garnering and clarifying strategic, operational, and tactical levels of support.

✪ Identifying employment requirements through contingency and crisis action planning.

✪ Defining levels of strategic and theater assets (prepositioned or for deployment).

✪ Accomplishing host-nation and coalition support agreements.

⊘ Establishing and maintaining deployment capabilities of resources through intratheater and intertheater movement.

⊘ Preparing for conflict termination and redeployment of forces.

To establish the sustainment of forces, planners must understand the joint community's concept of focused logistics. This concept seeks to replace the historical logistics emphasis on mass with a new emphasis on speed and precision through joint deployment and theater distribution.

Types of Planning and the Joint Operation Planning and Execution System (JOPES)

> *Planning for the employment of military forces is an inherent responsibility of command. Planning is performed at every echelon of command, and it is conducted across the range of military operations.*
>
> **—Joint Pub 5-0, Joint Operations Planning**

The Air Force recognizes the importance of the JOPES process to the warfighter. The JOPES process includes threat identification, strategy determination, COA development, detailed planning, and implementation. Contingency and crisis action planning are the primary operational planning activities described in JOPES, and they are implemented in the JOPP. The key component of these JOPES planning activities is the commander's estimate decision process.

There are two types of planning that are used to prepare for contingencies, briefly described below. See JP 5-0, *Joint Operations Planning*, for a full description of the joint operational planning process.

Contingency planning is the first type, which occurs in non-crisis situations. A contingency is a situation that likely would involve military forces in response to natural and man-made disasters, terrorists, subversives, military operations by foreign powers, or other situations as directed by the President or SecDef. The joint planning and execution community uses contingency planning to develop plans for a broad range of contingencies. Contingency planning facilitates the transition to CAP.

CAP is based on current events and conducted in time-sensitive situations and emergencies using assigned, attached, and allocated forces and resources. Crisis action planners base their plan on the actual circumstances that exist at the time planning occurs. They follow prescribed CAP procedures that parallel contingency planning, but are more flexible and responsive to changing events.

The Service component commands perform joint planning functions both within the chain of command and under the administrative control of the military departments. This is the role of the COMAFFOR and his/her AFFOR staff, primarily the A-5. Within the chain of command, the Service component commands recommend the proper force composition and employment of Service forces. They provide Service forces and support information for joint planning, and prepare component-level operation plans or OPORDs in support of taskings assigned to the combatant commands. Under their ADCON responsibilities, the Service component commands prepare and execute administrative and logistic plans to support operating forces.

The JOPP is a coordinated joint staff procedure used by commanders to determine the best method of accomplishing assigned tasks and to direct the actions necessary to accomplish those tasks. JOPES is used to conduct joint planning. JOPES facilitates the building and maintenance of OPLANs and concept plans, which are also referred to as OPLANS in concept format (CONPLANs) (with or without time phased force deployment data [TPFDD]). It aids in the development of effective options and OPORDs through adaptation of OPLANs or plan creation in a no-plan scenario. JOPES provides policies and procedures to ensure effective management of planning operations across the spectrum of mobilization, deployment, employment, sustainment, and redeployment. As part of the application suite approved to ride on the GCCS architecture, JOPES supports the deployment and transportation aspects of joint operation planning and execution. The Air Force uses JOPES, which then feeds the JOPP.

Each Service has its own war planning systems and databases. The Air Force war and mobilization plan (WMP) is published in six volumes. It provides major commands and Air Force staff agencies consolidated guidance concerning the support of combatant forces and mobilization planning. The WMP provides consolidated lists of OPLANs, lists of combat and support forces available to support OPLANs, planned positioning and use of aircraft forces in support of joint OPLANs, basic planning factors, and base use.

Once the contingency planning or CAP process is completed, a number of COAs are presented to the JFC, who then decides on one COA (or a combination of COAs). The selected COA is then refined and disseminated to commanders for further planning and execution by their respective component staffs.

COA Selection and AOC and AFFOR Staff Interface

Commanders select a COA (or multiple COAs) for operations to commence. This is part of command responsibility, to provide guidance for subordinates. Once a COA is selected, the JFC then develops an OPORD that describes the COA and tasks supporting commanders to implement the approved COA. The primary purpose of the OPORD is to provide guidance and direction to subordinate units. The Service component of commands (in this case, the COMAFFOR) develops Service aspects of the COA, determines force and resource requirements, and builds TPFDDs to implement the deployment aspects of the COA. The COMAFFOR also works within Service channels to identify combat support forces, critical materiel, sustaining supplies, filler and replacement personnel, and reserve component asset availability.

As the JFC develops the OPORD prior to execution, subordinate Service and functional components (in this case, the COMAFFOR) are also tasked to develop supporting plans and/or OPORDs. These products should then be cross-walked by the JFC staff to ensure integration. Simultaneously and in coordination, the AFFOR Staff, usually led by the A-5, will develop an Air Force component supporting plan or OPORD to capture information pertinent to Air Force forces deploying to and employing within the particular area of operations.

The Service component supporting plan or OPORD should follow JOPES formats and be comprehensive enough to cover all combat support aspects of how the Air Force will fight. The Service OPORD may overlap the CFACC's JAOP—the sole employment plan for air and space component forces—in some respects, but this may be necessary to give appropriate guidance to the AFFOR staff where their duties differ from those of the CFACC's AOC staff. Although contingency planning may provide many rich samples of theater planning, often the OPORD or supporting plan developed must now reflect the reality of the situation (since many of the contingency planning assumptions are no longer assumed or necessarily valid).

This OPORD should include a basic plan plus appropriate annexes and appendices. Ownership of the annexes and appendices is divided among the AFFOR staff; and, once developed and approved, should be made available to all Air Force units within the AETF for execution. See AFDD 2 for an expanded discussion of the Air Force component planning process.

DIRECTING

Directing is giving specific instructions and guidance to subordinate units. Superior commanders often give specific instructions to subordinates on mission objectives, situation, resources, and acceptable risks. Commanders should also give their guidance or "intent" to subordinates as a way to encourage initiative and reduce the uncertainty throughout the spectrum of conflict. Direction is guidance to or management of support staff functions, inherent within command but not a command authority in its own right. In some cases, direction can be considered an explicit instruction or order. It is used by commanders and their designated subordinates to facilitate, channel, or motivate support staff to achieve appropriate action, tempo, or intensity. It is used by directors of staff agencies on behalf of the commander to provide guidance to their staffs on how best to accomplish stated objectives in accordance with the commander's intent.

COORDINATING

Coordinating is sharing information to gain consensus, explain tasks, and optimize operations. To ensure required support is available, coordination in advance of execution is critical. Commanders should ensure the shared information (both vertical and horizontal) produces trusting relationships and gains agreements necessary for efficient multinational and joint operations. Coordination is defined as the necessary action to ensure adequate exchange of information to integrate, synchronize, and deconflict operations between separate organizations. Its benefits include minimizing risk of fratricide; ensuring adequate exchange of information to integrate, synchronize, and deconflict operations between separate organizations; and mutual exchange of information. Coordination is not necessarily a process of gaining approval but is most often used for mutual exchange of information. It is normally used between functions of a supporting staff. DIRLAUTH is used to coordinate with an organization outside of the immediate staff or organization, or between component staffs. Although each component of a joint force develops its own plan as part of the JFC's overall effort, these plans are most successful if they are coordinated among the Service components. Plans should be coordinated with as much time as possible before execution, to ensure all required support is coordinated for the operation.

CONTROLLING

Controlling is a composite function that uses parts of the planning, directing, and coordinating processes to ensure efficient execution of operations. Controlling requires current information to produce feedback. Feedback is essential to correct errant results or to issue new orders that exploit advantages. Controlling involves a means to disseminate guidance and to influence ongoing and future operations. Controlling operations or processes may span the spectrum from involvement in every aspect to giving generalized guidance to achieve a result. The span of control given to subordinates depends on the situation, the personality of the commander, and the confidence the commander has in the subordinate to carry out the task.

ASSESSING

Assessing is determining the nature and impact of conditions and events to include the military implications of intelligence indicators, environmental effects, and orders of battle. It implies ability to develop situational awareness, evaluate threats and opportunities and to provide early warning and attack assessment to:

✪ Determine and assess the nature and impact of critical events in the operational environment.

✪ Assess status of resources.

✪ Assess the impact of environmental factors on operations.

✪ Assess termination options, conditions, and proposals.

✪ Assess implications of fused, all source intelligence.

✪ Assess events relative to ROE, treaties, and agreements.

✪ Conduct effects-based assessment in order to adapt effects and taskings to execute operations in the future.

CHAPTER FIVE

TECHNOLOGY ATTRIBUTES AND DEVELOPING C2 PROFESSIONALS

> *War is a matter of vital importance to the state, the province of life or death, the road to survival or ruin. It is mandatory that it be thoroughly studied.*
>
> **—Sun Tzu, The Art of War**

People, processes, and effective use of available technology enable successful C2 for military operations. Processes were discussed previously. This chapter discusses the other two central themes that affect C2. One theme, the *technology* element, covers the equipment, communications, and facilities needed to overcome the warfighting problems of integrating actions across space and time. Technology elements tend to dominate C2 doctrine, because advanced technology characterizes American warfare. Technology attributes are important and must be understood before C2 operations can be conducted effectively. The other theme, *personnel*, covers the human aspects of C2, including the requirement to develop C2 professionals to meet the complex global requirements of today's military operations. Personnel, technology, and processes must all come together to efficiently execute C2 functions.

JP 6-0, *Joint Communications System*, states: "The objective of the joint communications system is to facilitate the proper integration and employment of joint force operational capabilities through effective command and control." It also must ensure the continuous, automated flow and processing of information. The joint C2 system must be interoperable, reliable, mobile, disciplined, survivable, and sustainable. These principles provide the foundation on which the Services build their systems and are applied during planning and execution of military operations. The C2 system provides the JFC with the ability to control the flow and processing of information. It supports the JFC's decision-making process and provides him/her with the capability to achieve the desired effects during joint operations.

In accordance with guidelines and direction from the SecDef, each military department or Service, as appropriate, has the following common functions and responsibilities pertaining to joint operations:

✪ To provide flexibility, as required, to meet changing situations and diversified operations with minimum disruption or delay.

✪ To provide interoperable and compatible C2 systems, warfighters, and reserves of equipment and supplies for the effective prosecution of war and to plan for the expansion of peacetime communications to meet the needs of war.

✪ To provide, organize, train, and equip its C2 systems personnel and provide interoperable and compatible C2 systems equipment for joint operations.

✪ To install, operate, and maintain assigned facilities of the DISN, including the capability of meeting the provisions of applicable standards.

✪ To maintain mobile, transportable C2 system assets, which are controlled by the CJCS, in a high state of readiness.

The Services must provide C2 systems that can support joint operations. This is established as part of their mission to train and equip personnel and forces to be employed by the JFC. When forces are deployed for a contingency, it is too late to discover that C2 systems do not meet the characteristics discussed below. Failure to achieve joint standards among C2 systems will result in system degradation, if not mission failure. Coalition C2 system characteristics and requirements must also be considered during system procurement and in contingency planning.

INTEROPERABILITY

Interoperability is the ability of C2 systems to exchange information, allowing warfighters to operate effectively together. Interoperability is best achieved by adhering to technology and process standards that allow information flow. Unity of command is difficult, if not impossible, to achieve when C2 systems do not work together. In the past, most C2 systems were designed strictly to meet the needs of a particular Service or functional commander. This is changing. However, the focus on multinational operations will continue to challenge us, particularly in security issues and technology gaps. Every effort should be made to share the needed information efficiently among the multinational forces participating in an operation.

Numerous directives require the Services to migrate existing Service- or function-specific C2 systems and applications to a standard defense information infrastructure (DII). This infrastructure is not a C2 system, but provides a common operating environment (COE) or a foundation for building where functionality is added or removed in small, manageable segments. To achieve interoperability, the DOD established the joint technical architecture (JTA) and the communications systems support (CSS) architectural framework. The framework implements a standard DOD architecture

USAF C2 systems must be interoperable with joint and combined systems.

that provides the needed structure while systems are in the developmental and system engineering phases of acquisition. The JTA identifies a common set of mandatory information technology standards and guidelines to be used for sending, receiving, understanding, and processing information.

RELIABILITY AND REDUNDANCY

Redundant C2 systems provide the ability for alternative C2 systems to continue operations in the event of failure or damage to the primary system. C2 system redundancy begins with planning. Redundancy requirements should balance the goal of mission success against natural failures. High value C2 systems that are difficult to back up, such as the AOC, are good candidates for redundancy planning. A COMAFFOR should plan for redundancy by using distributed C2 operations. For example, the commander could designate the alternate AOC or another NAF's AOC as backup. This backup plan must be formalized by a set of agreements and specified in the OPLAN. It should also be exercised before military operations commence.

The Three Segments of Communications Connectivity

The "first 400 feet" is what the customer actually sees. It consists of those applications, the environment, services, and functionality used to train, organize and equip the user on a daily basis. This includes elements deployed as part of a C2 element, such as the AOC or possibly a flying squadron. The first 400 feet involve software and hardware applications that the customers see every day, including the desktop computers, FAX machines, telephones, and radios at the users' fingertips. The first 400 feet also include behind-the-scenes services such as processing imagery devices that tie the customers' instruments together forming a network. This network interfaces with realms beyond the first 400 feet.

There is also the segment known as "inside the gate," or the base information infrastructure (BII). This provides an information utility between users and from users to the GIG. Services include on-site voice and data networks, protection of the networks from intrusion, official and unofficial electronic messaging, spectrum management, and interface to the global grid. Inside the gate systems may tie the ICC and individual squadrons together, as an example.

The last segment, "outside the gate," connects to the GIG. Depending on its scope, this realm may be considered the global, defense, or theater information infrastructure. Regardless of its name, the outside the gate realm, in conjunction with the first 400 feet and inside the gate realms, tie together a system of systems to create the global grid. This element ties together the AOC-forward with the AOC-rear or lateral or subordinate C2 nodes, to enable reachback, as well as support for the COMAFFOR and JFC from all aspects of the GIG.

—Multiple Sources

COMMUNICATIONS CAPABILITIES

Commanders must have access to information. This information is required for them to exercise Air Force distinctive capabilities. **Commanders must be provided with tools for decision-making through effective control, exploitation, and protection of information regardless of form or function.** The objective of communications and information services is to create a global and transparent interface to C2 centers and to provide users with the information necessary to carry out the mission. Commanders are provided a connection to the C2 centers through a common operating environment, collectively referred to as the GIG. A useful construct is to consider the C2 centers and their users as being divided into three segments or realms for communications connectivity: the "Last 400 Feet," "Inside the Gate," "and Outside the Gate," as described above.

USEABLE DATA FOR DECISION-MAKING

Commanders must have actionable information that has been sorted and processed. Today's information systems can process huge amounts of data and forward that data in near-real time. During a contingency, a commander usually cannot sort through a vast amount of data. There is simply too much data available and not enough time. The commander's staff must analyze and sift through the data to forward information the commander actually needs to enable a decision. There is a concern that commanders and staffs will suffer from "information overload." They could miss the truly important nugget of information while sorting through a mountain of data. The human element will always be required in the decision-making process.

KEY NETWORKS

C2 throughout the DOD relies on a series of networks to provide conduits for the rapid exchange of information among nodes. The networks are provided under the aegis of DISA or DIA, but individual network facilities are furnished, installed, operated, and maintained by one or another of the Service or functional components. For network facilities to be interoperable, they must adhere to protocol and performance standards established by DISA or DIA. The result is consistent, seamless, robust, and redundant data exchange service available to warfighters worldwide. Figure 5.1 presents a representative sample of key networks supporting the warfighter.

Communications Planning

Communications planning is an essential element of effective C2. The need to communicate effectively demands that planners analyze the commander's requirements and translate those needs into workable solutions. These needs are normally met by installing a combination of organic and commercial communications systems prioritized to effectively support the commander's tasking. The goal is to maximize the use of organic military capabilities and expand with commercial systems to increase capacity and reliability and to generate greater freedom of action.

Network	Long Title	Purpose	Applications Supported
NIPRNET	Non-secure Internet Protocol Router Network	Unclassified data exchange. Internet access.	E-mail, browser-based data mining, GCSS, AFMSS, dissemination of public information, collaborative tools, office applications, DMS
SIPRNET	Secret Internet Protocol Router Network	Classified data exchange. Command and control.	GCCS, GCSS, AFMSS, TBMCS, JDISS, Intelink-S, collaborative tools, office applications, desktop VTC, E-mail, DMS
JWICS	Joint Worldwide Intelligence Communications System (also an Internet Protocol Router Network)	SCI Exchange	JDISS, Intelink, Intel applications, VTC, E-mail, collaborative tools, office applications, DMS
DSN	Defense Switched Network	Telephone Service	Unclassified voice, facsimile, dial-in computer data transfer. Secure services via STU-III or STE.
DRSN	Defense Red Switched Network	Secure Telephone Service	Classified voice, video, fax and data.

Figure 5.1. Key Networks Supporting the Warfighter.

Modes of Communications Between C2 Systems

The primary means of communications between C2 nodes are voice and data. Principal transmission should be through secure and anti-jam communications equipment. Air Force C2 nets use fixed communications, leased communications and space-based communications capabilities for mission accomplishment. Theater communications capabilities include line of sight and satellite systems, but planners should also ensure that radio relays are considered to enhance over-the-horizon radio communications.

Joint Data Network

The Joint Data Network (JDN) allows connectivity between joint commanders, staffs, and components. It is a network comprised of four subnetworks, each of which is optimized to enable certain joint warfighting capabilities. The complexity of the JDN is significant, and an effective JDN plan is a key consideration in the overall planning process. Planners include combatant commands, JTF, and component command staffs, in coordination with the supporting services. Responsibility for implementation and management of each of the JDN subnetworks is normally assigned as depicted in Figure 5.2.

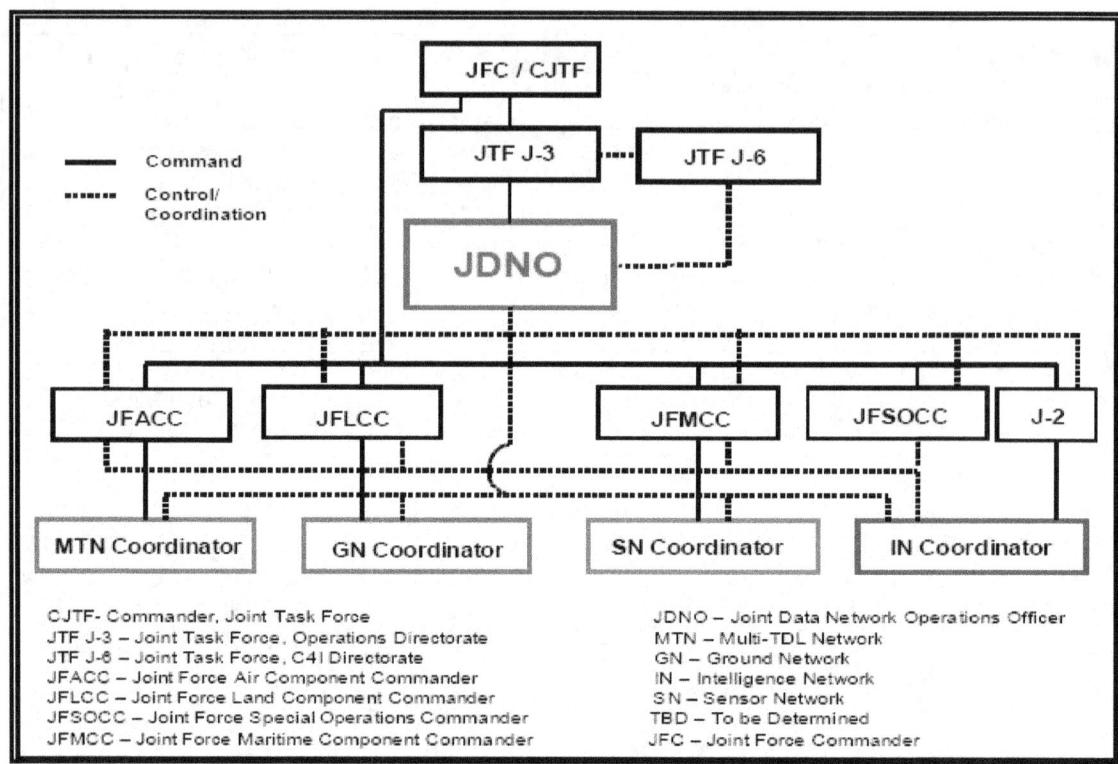

Figure 5.2 Organization for JDN Operations.

Tactical Digital Information Links and Gateways

Tactical Digital Information Links (TADLs) (also referred to as TADILs) are standardized communication links, approved by the JCS, suitable for transmission of digital information. All Services, including the Air Force, use these links to support their doctrinal requirements to exchange data and information quickly and in a readily recognizable format. These links support many missions, including air defense, airspace control, and the exchange of ISR data. Link 16 has been designated as the primary data link for use in the combat air forces. Some examples of data links are:

○ Army Tactical Data Link 1.

○ Link-11/11B (TADIL A/TADIL B).

○ Link 14 (Maritime, UHF or HF).

○ Link 16 (TADIL J).

CJCSM 6120.01C, *Joint Multi-Tactical Data Link Operating Procedures,* provides a detailed description of each link shown above.

Other tools exist for extending the TADL network. The situation awareness data link (SADL) integrates Air Force close air support aircraft with the digitized battlefield via the Army's enhanced position location reporting system. It provides fighter-to-fighter and air-to-ground/ground-to-air secure communications. The data link gateway is a

Navy system that provides TADL connectivity to a wide variety of users. Ships, aircraft, ADA units and fixed C2 sites use either a host emulator or a terminal emulator to pass data via TADIL J links, if not TADIL J-equipped. Some AETACS and GTACS elements have this capability. The data link gateway can also be used for exercises and for operational training.

Installation Mapping and Visualization for C2 Operations

Commanders and planners use a common installation picture for mission success. Installations represent the underlying platform for AF missions. Installation operations also require disciplined creation, management, and sharing of critical georeferenced information through modern mapping processes. The AFSPC GeoBase program satisfies this critical need across the installation mission spectrum.

The GeoBase program provides a data service, referred to as the "GeoBase Service," that can be simultaneously accessed and exploited on Air Force networks by any number of base and higher headquarters organizations. Installation maps (geospatial data) are made available via the service to provide a single point of access for visualizing installation situations, conditions, assets, and facilities. The GeoBase service may be fused with functional automated information systems and other information and technology solutions providing the ability to view functional information assets via the base map.

TESTING, CERTIFICATION, AND SECURITY REQUIREMENTS FOR C2 SYSTEMS

C2 systems have certain requirements that must be met before they can be placed into service. These requirements are spelled out in DOD directives that govern the acquisition process. The DOD information technology security certification and accreditation process (DITSCAP) is composed of four phases: definition, verification, validation, and post accreditation. Phase 1, definition, is focused on understanding the mission, environment, and architecture to determine the security requirements and level of effort necessary to achieve accreditation. Phase 2, verification, verifies the evolving or modified system's compliance with the information agreed on in the systems security authorization agreements (SSAA) that govern the requirements process. Phase 3, validation, validates compliance of the fully integrated system with the information stated in the SSAA. Phases 1, 2, and 3 are repeated as often as necessary to produce an accredited system. Phase 4, post accreditation, includes those activities necessary for the continuing operation of the accredited information technology system in its computing environment and to address the changing threats a system faces through its life cycle. Phase 4 starts after the system has been certified and accredited for operations. The objectives of phase 4 are to ensure secure system management, operation, and maintenance to preserve an acceptable level of residual risk. Once certified, the C2 system is ready for employment.

C2 SYSTEMS CHARACTERISTICS

The fundamental purpose of C2 systems is to ensure commanders receive mission-essential information, make informed and timely decisions, and communicate appropriate commands to subordinates throughout the operation. To achieve this purpose, C2 systems must meet the cost, schedule, and performance criteria set during the requirements phase of the acquisition process. In establishing these requirements, users and developers must also ensure C2 systems are interoperable, sustainable, and survivable. For C2 systems to be effective they must be:

- ✪ Flexible. Required to meet changing situations and diversified operations with minimum disruption or delay.

- ✪ Responsive. Able to respond instantaneously to demands for information; must be reliable, redundant, and timely.

- ✪ Mobile. Must be as mobile as the forces, elements, or organizations they support without degraded information quality or flow.

- ✪ Disciplined. The C2 infrastructure must be focused, balanced, and based on predetermined needs for critical information.

- ✪ Survivable. National policy dictates the survivability of national command centers and the communications systems through which decisions are transmitted to forces.

- ✪ Sustainable. Must provide continuous support during any type and length of operations; requires economical design and employment.

- ✪ Interoperable. Should be able to operate with key joint and coalition C2 systems.

Threats to C2 Systems

A distributed network, such as the GIG, feeds on shared information, over a robust communications network. The GIG relies on a global grid of linked US and allied military and multinational commercial networks and communications systems for its inputs. This grid, along with advanced sensors and automation, enables information sharing and thus information superiority.

The threat to a network, such as the GIG, is two-fold. First, since the system feeds on information, an enemy can target the distributed network with robust IO. Because of the inexpensive nature of this threat, even the weakest adversary is capable of conducting an aggressive campaign to infiltrate, corrupt, disrupt, and neutralize information flow. This capability produces an asymmetric relationship in any future conflict. No matter how strong our military forces may be, a capable IO adversary could adversely affect our C2 capability if we are not fully protected.

The second threat is to our communications links. The GIG provides robust, redundant communications. We must always be vigilant for a potential adversary attempting to disrupt our communications links, whether they are provided through purely military means or through increased use of the civilian communications sector. Further, future space capabilities of foreign powers may require increased attention to air and space superiority, as our space-based platforms are critical to successful distributed operations. The design of the GIG must also contain enough redundancy so that single points of failure do not present themselves as lucrative targets to an adversary.

There is also the threat of physical violence, either through conventional attack or terrorist activity. One aspect of distributed operations is to present a smaller forward C2 presence in order to minimize risk. However, there is always a risk, even to forces in the US, and therefore force protection will continue to be a major concern for the commander. The operational and communications architecture should be designed with sufficient reliability, redundancy, and protections to ensure robust operation and minimal degradation. This facet should be exercised regularly in training events for the C2 system.

Threats to C2 systems, including information systems, can come from a variety of sources. Adversaries include hostile nations, groups, or individuals, and may include domestic threats. Specific threats to C2 systems may consist of the operations/activities shown below:

✪ Masquerading. Also known as attempting to gain access by posing as an authorized user. Information assurance programs, password selection, use, and protection are vital to counter these intrusions.

✪ Network attack. The employment of network-based capabilities to destroy, disrupt, corrupt, or usurp information resident in or transiting through networks. Networks include telephony and data service networks.

✪ Spoofing. The insertion of data causing a system to inadvertently disclose information or data.

✪ Electronic warfare (EW). EW can cause denial of service and corruption of data by employing electromagnetic energy. Electromagnetic pulses can corrupt and destroy data stored on magnetic media and damage software and hardware.

✪ Other operations/activities revealed by foreign intelligence. Foreign intelligence can provide information in support of other threats. It can provide insight into communications infrastructure and information transfer techniques. Foreign intelligence is an all-source threat that includes signals intelligence, human intelligence, and possibly other sources.

✪ Substitution and modification. This disrupts planning and operations by modifying or substituting false data or information in a system. The objective can be to influence a specific plan or operation, and shake the user's faith in the integrity of his/her information.

✪ Physical attacks. Physical attacks or destruction because of natural disaster can be a threat to information systems. Facilities and physical resources may be lost, and the loss of connectivity can be devastating.

✪ Unauthorized access. Access to any computer, network, storage medium, system, program, file, data, user area, or other private repository, without the express permission of the owner.

Network Defense and Network Operations Organizations

NetD and Network Operations (NETOPS) organizations provide US forces with critical capabilities to realize the effects of information and decision superiority. Collectively, these organizations provide varying degrees of NetD and NETOPS support. They provide commanders with real-time intrusion detection and perimeter defense capabilities, network management and fault resolution activities, data fusion, assessment, and decision support. During employment, organizations are arranged into a three-tiered operational hierarchy which facilitates synchronized application of their collective capabilities in support of DOD's defense-in-depth security strategy. This defense-in-depth approach employs and integrates the abilities of people, operations, and technology to establish multilayer, multidimensional protection. Security and protection include policies and programs to help counter internal and external threats— whether foreign or domestic—to include protection against trusted insider misconduct or error. For more information on NetD and NETOPS organizations, see AFDD 2-5, *Information Operations.*

Information Assurance (IA)

IA is a key enabler of C2 capabilities. IA comprises those measures taken to protect and defend information and information systems by ensuring their availability, integrity, authenticity, confidentiality, and non-repudiation (ability to prove sender's identity and prove delivery to recipient). IA depends on the continuous integration of trained personnel, operational and technical capabilities, and necessary policies and procedures to guarantee continuous and dependable information, while providing the means to efficiently reconstitute these vital services following disruptions of any kind, whether from an attack, natural disaster, equipment failure, or operator error. In an assured information environment, C2 professionals and other warfighters can leverage the power of the information age.

Developing and implementing security and protection in the 21st Century requires recognition of the globalization of information and information systems. *Security, like interoperability, must be incorporated into information systems designs from the beginning to be effective and affordable.* Levels of protection must be commensurate to the importance and vulnerability of the specific information and information systems. An IMP is effective in developing IA capabilities, but will also speed the transfer of critical information. It will route information in the most expeditious manner throughout the C2 system. Internal and external attack threats must be anticipated as a part of the IMP. The various types of threats include:

✪ Hacker. An unauthorized user who attempts to or gains access to an information system with intent to cause malicious destruction of data.

✪ Disgruntled system users. Authorized users with malicious intent who abuse the system.

✪ Poor communications security (COMSEC), computer security, and operations security practices.

✪ Viruses (malicious code).

✪ Unauthorized/unintentional disclosure of data. This threat increases proportionally to the Air Force's use of automation.

✪ Corruption of data. This is an insidious method of deception, which, if undetected, leads to faulty guidance, coordination, decision-making, and execution.

✪ Physical disruption or denial of communications. This threat can be internally or externally generated.

✪ Terrorist groups.

✪ State sponsored information attacks.

Protection and defense of information and information systems is accomplished through aggressive application of IA measures. The predominant means to apply IA is through information security, which could include intrusion detection, effective isolation, and incident response to restore information and system security. Vigilance must be maintained when securing any form of information medium or communication system. The dynamic nature of the developing information environment requires well-developed IA programs to ensure effective information management (IM).

Education programs for information security are essential for Airmen, enabling them to conduct their duties in today's complex technological environment. Traditional programs such as COMSEC, physical security, emissions security, and NetD are methods to protect our information and information systems. In addition, other IA programs help assess the interoperability, compatibility, and supportability of our information systems and aim specifically to reduce vulnerabilities and to improve the overall security of shared networks and systems. Due to the US dependency on and the general vulnerability of information and its supporting systems, IA is essential to effective C2 operations.

A well crafted and coordinated set of integrated, interoperable procedures are of great importance, considering the increasing joint and multinational context of current and future operations. The value of technology, organization, and strategy is diminished in the absence of a professional force to leverage their value. To meet uncertain challenges on the horizon, that force must be fully indoctrinated in employment of joint and multinational warfighting capabilities. They must also be trained to embody the inherent adaptability required to react to and counter the dynamics of an asymmetric operational environment. A comprehensive and thoroughly rehearsed library of operational procedures is crucial to developing that required degree of proficiency. Information systems and networks must be of sufficient scale, capacity, reach, and reliability to support evolving operational and training missions.

Information Management

An effective plan and operating procedures for handling information are an asset to commanders and all members of the task force. C2 is essentially about information: getting it, judging its value, processing it into useful form, acting on it, and sharing it with others. There are two basic uses for information. The first is to help create situational awareness as the basis for a decision. The second is to direct and coordinate actions in the execution of the decision. The C2 system must present information in a form that is both quickly understood and useful to the recipient. Many sources of information are imperfect and susceptible to distortion and deception.

Combining pieces of information with context produces ideas or provides knowledge. C2 is as much a problem of IM as it is of carrying out other warfighting tasks. Good IM makes accomplishment of other tasks less complex. Automation and standardization of communications system processes and procedures improve IM and assist the commander's effectiveness and speed of C2. Today, improved technology in mobility, weapons, sensors, and communications continues to reduce reaction time, increase the tempo of operations, and generate large amounts of information. If information is not well managed the reactions of commanders and decision makers and ultimately the joint force may be degraded. It is essential the communications system complement human capabilities and reduce or eliminate known limitations. Effective IM procedures need to be promulgated through the IMP and lessons learned need to be retained for future reference.

Effective IM is everyone's responsibility. All personnel are information managers. IM includes all processes involved in the creation, receipt, collection, control, dissemination, storage, retrieval, protection, and disposition of information. As an information user, each Airman has inherent responsibilities to acquire, assess, reason, question, correlate, fuse, place in context, and disseminate quality information to others.

IM procedures must be established by the operational community to enhance, exploit, and use the concept of distributed operations. Also, more effective use of existing bandwidth will result in better communications capability. Protocols for the timing and detail of information will eliminate a constant influx of information that tends to overwhelm the warfighter. Operators must decide early on exactly what information they require, and publish the rules for information exchange, then enforce the rules with information discipline.

Information Quality Criteria

The criteria shown below help characterize information quality. By applying these criteria, the danger of the commander and staff receiving too much information, or undigested or inaccurate information, can be mitigated. For information to be useful to the commander it must be:

✪ Accurate. It must convey the true situation.

✪ Relevant. It must apply to the mission, task, or situation ahead.

✪ Timely. It must be available in time to make decisions.

✪ Usable. It must be in a common, easily understood format and display.

✪ Complete. It must reflect all necessary information required by the decision maker.

✪ Brief. It must contain only the level of detail that is required.

✪ Secure. It must be afforded adequate protection where required.

The Importance of Information Systems Protection

Mission accomplishment depends on protecting and defending information and information systems from destruction, disruption, corruption, and safeguarding from intrusion and exploitation. Everyone should assume his or her information and information system is a target. Therefore, all users share responsibility for adequately protecting and defending friendly information and information systems.

The success or failure of the JFC's mission depends on his/her ability to have accurate and timely information available to the decision makers. The objective of this IM plan is to map all processes involved to synergistically function to deliver decision-ready information to the AOC or other C2 node. As such, the right information needs to be given to the right person at the right time in the right format and level of detail needed for commanders to make the right decision positively affecting planning and execution of air and space operations.

DEVELOPING AIR FORCE C2 PROFESSIONALS

A global C2 system requires a trained cadre of professionals to operate and to support the full range of military operations. **Specialized training and education of C2 professionals improves combat effectiveness; makes C2 capabilities universally understood, accepted, and exploitable by joint forces; and creates military and civilian C2 experts and leaders with a stronger foundation in force employment and capabilities.** Some C2 nodes, such as a combat control team, have personnel assigned as crew members from a small and specialized career field. These individuals bring unique training and experience to their C2 nodes. They will probably spend an entire career applying their knowledge supporting C2 operations worldwide. Other C2 nodes, such as an AOC, have a broad cross-section of Air Force specialties in their crew composition. Many positions in the AOC and other C2 nodes are filled by personnel who do not necessarily have a "C2" core Air Force specialty code. They may be trained as navigators or intelligence specialists, for example. These personnel may only be assigned to the AOC or other C2 node for one tour. They must become fully proficient in C2 operations while in that crew position to effectively and safely execute today's complex military operations.

C2 operators function in war within an environment that cannot be precisely duplicated in peacetime. Therefore, realistic training on actual C2 operational equipment is critical to developing personnel with the judgment, experience, and instincts necessary to effectively perform C2 tasks. People, technology elements, and processes make C2 a force enhancer. *Commanders must ensure their people are fully proficient at using designated C2 systems when performing wartime duties.* Consequently, C2 professionals should be trained and educated in the manner they intend to fight. This should include training, education, and exercise scenarios that simulate potential real world situations, as well as experiments and wargames that consider the broader implications of future conflict.

TRAINING AIR FORCE C2 PROFESSIONALS

C2 professionals should be trained throughout their careers to provide effective C2 of forces across the range of military operations and during all phases of an operation. Continual training is crucial to maintain proficiency because C2 forces, along with the forces they control and their tactics, techniques, and procedures are constantly evolving. In concert with training, evaluation is essential to identifying shortfalls and is a critical measure of training program effectiveness. Most C2 professionals function as part of a team. Experience gained in a variety of real world operations is always a plus in forming a crew or team of C2 professionals. It is not possible to outline the career track of each C2 career field in this or any other single document. There are, however, certain stages of training and career progression common to all C2 professionals.

Accession, Initial Qualification, and Mission Qualification Training

Accession training establishes the basis for all future learning. Training C2 professionals should begin in accession programs. Here the trainee gains knowledge and an appreciation for air and space operations in the context of overall Air Force and joint operations. C2 professionals learn their operating skills through initial qualification training (IQT). Formal C2 systems training and education begin with basic instruction on fundamental C2 competencies. C2 professionals receive IQT in their specific mission system. Mission qualification training (MQT) prepares C2 professionals for mission ready certification. MQT should include training by unit instructors on both operational systems and in exercises, if possible. The ultimate purpose of MQT is to prepare the C2 professionals to accomplish all tasks associated with their particular mission and to ready them for their mission ready evaluation and certification. MQT is supplemented by the owning command for theater-specific and local area procedures to ensure that C2 professionals are prepared to execute operations in their assigned area of responsibility.

Continuation Training

Continuation training is proficiency or recurring training that ensures C2 professionals remain adept in their skills and current in their knowledge. To maintain proficiency, they receive recurring training on all tasks required to perform their jobs, even those that may only be required on a periodic basis. If operators fail to demonstrate a required level of proficiency, they should receive individual training to correct any deficient areas. Additionally, supplemental training may be required when warranted by new procedures, hardware, or software affecting operational equipment. All categories of proficiency training (recurring, individual, and supplemental) may include classroom instruction, simulations, or hands-on training with an operational C2 system.

Operational Level Training

Advanced training covers any specific training in unique aspects of the operational mission. Once C2 professionals are declared mission ready they may receive advanced training to assure their proficiency in activities involving instruction, evaluation, or special mission requirements. For example, the Air Force weapons school provides advanced tactical-level training to select C2 personnel on the conduct and integration of C2 capabilities with theater operations. Those weapons school graduates then become subject matter experts in employing their respective weapon system and teach others in the operational art and provide updates on tactics.

Training for Air Force C2 professionals extends from application of tactical procedures in a specific environment to understanding the principles involved in commanding forces across a theater of operations. C2 professionals should progress through levels of training commensurate with their levels of command or positions as a staff member or a key adviser to a functional commander. An appreciation of C2 capabilities and requirements for operations across the full range of military operations is the goal for the training and education process for the C2 professional.

Senior personnel such as the COMAFFOR, the CFACC, their staffs, and other personnel may require training to accomplish specific missions. These senior officers and their staffs must be able to execute critical C2 functions both in peacetime and during contingencies. Peacetime training opportunities afford the greatest environment to learn the art of effective C2, with the least impact on real world operations and in a permissive and forgiving learning environment.

C2 warrior training is one form of operational training offered at the 505th Command and Control Wing located at Hurlburt Field, Florida, and other locations. This training, while initially focused at the AOC staff, is rapidly evolving into a standard training curriculum for the C2 personnel who must staff and employ C2 centers.

The C2 warrior training will be relevant in the near term to operational-level C2, but is useful to those C2 personnel who man tactical-level nodes as well. The joint air ground operations group at Nellis AFB, Nevada, also conducts training in tactical C2 processes, notably for TACP and ASOC personnel.

Commanders and Development of C2 Professionals

Stringent standards of performance should be established to ensure C2 professionals attain and maintain the high degree of proficiency required for mission success. Commanders at all levels should be involved with the training and evaluation of their personnel and should ensure they meet minimum standards before being certified mission ready.

In my travels around the world, foreign political and military leaders continually ask how we field such a talented, dedicated, and capable enlisted corps. Our enlisted corps is the envy of the world, and is a major reason we have emerged as the most respected air and space force on the planet. This is no accident. Over the years, we've invested heavily in our Airmen—in training, education, and benefits. We've reaped the rewards of these investments many times over, in war and peace. As we face new challenges, it's imperative we continue to evolve the processes we use to develop Airmen. We must ensure our development opportunities produce the skills needed to remain the world's premier enlisted air and space force.

**—General John P. Jumper,
CSAF, 2001-2005**

At the very heart of warfare lies doctrine....

Suggested Readings

Air Force Publications (Note: All Air Force doctrine documents are available on the Air Force Doctrine Center web page at **https://www.doctrine.af.mil**)

AFDD 1, *Air Force Basic Doctrine*

AFDD 1-1, *Leadership and Force Development*

AFDD 2, *Operations and Organization*

AFDD 2-1.5, *Nuclear Operations*

AFDD 2-1.7, *Airspace Control in the Combat Zone*

AFDD 2-2, *Space Operations*

AFDD 2-4, *Combat Support*

AFDD 2-5, *Information Operations*

AFDD 2-6, *Air Mobility Operations*

AFDD 2-7, *Special Operations*

AFDD 2-10, *Homeland Security Operations*

AFI 10-207, *Command Posts*

AFI 10-2701, *Organization and Function of the Civil Air Patrol*

AFI 13-1AOC, Vol. 3, *Operational Procedures-Air and Space Operations Center*

AFI 38-101, *Air Force Organizations*

AFI 51-604, *Appointment to and Assumption of Command*

AFOTTP 2-3.2, *Air and Space Operations Center*

AFTTP 3-1, Vol. 26, *Theater Air Control System*

The US Air Force Transformation Flight Plan, Deputy Chief of Staff for Plans and Programs; Future Concepts and Transformation Division, U.S. Air Force, November, 2003.

Joint Publications

JP 0-2, *Unified Action Armed Forces (UNAAF)*

JP 1, *Joint Warfare of the Armed Forces of the United States*

JP 1-02, *Department of Defense Dictionary of Military and Associated Terms*

JP 3-0, *Joint Operations*

JP 3-01, *Countering Air and Missile Threats*

JP 3-16, *Joint Doctrine for Multinational Operations*

JP 3-30, *Command and Control for Joint Air Operations*

JP 5-0, *Joint Operations Planning*

JP 6-0, *Joint Communications System*

Department of Defense Publications

DODD 5100.1, *Functions of the Department of Defense and its Major Components*

DODI 5200.40, *DOD Information Technology Security Certification and Accreditation Process (DITSCAP)*

The Implementation of Network-Centric Warfare, Director, Force Transformation, Office of the Secretary of Defense, Washington, D.C. 2005.

Other Publications

Articles

Griffith, Thomas E, Colonel, USAF. *Command Relations at the Operational Level of War Kenney, MacArthur, and Arnold.* Airpower Journal, Summer 1999.

Books

Alberts, David E., and Richard E. Hayes. *Power to the Edge, Command and Control in the Information Age.* Command and Control Research Program, Office of the Assistant Secretary of Defense (NII). 2003.

Clausewitz, Carl von, *On War*, trans. and ed., Michael Howard and Peter Paret. Princeton University Press. 1984.

Clodfelter, Richard, *The Limits of Airpower* (Free Press). 1989.

Coakley, Thomas P., *Command and Control for War and Peace*, (NDU Press). 1992.

Cole, Ronald H., *Operation URGENT FURY, Grenada, The Planning and Execution of Joint Operations in Grenada, 12 October - 2 November 1983*. Joint History Office, Office of the Chairman of the Joint Chiefs of Staff Washington, DC. 1997.

Davis, Richard G., *Carl A. Spaatz and the Air War in Europe*. (DC). 1992.

Gordon, Michael R., and Trainor, Bernard E., Lieutenant General USMC (Retired). *The General's War*. (Little Brown and Company). 1995.

Grant, Rebecca., *The First 600 Days of Combat: The US Air Force in the Global War on Terrorism*. (IRIS Press). 2004.

Hallion, Richard P., *Storm Over Iraq, Air Power and the Gulf War*. (Smithsonian Institution Press). 1992.

Kenney, George C., General. *General Kenney Reports*. (DC). 1987.

Owen, Robert C., Colonel, USAF. *Deliberate Force, A Case Study in Effective Air Campaigning*. (Air University Press). 2000.

Patton, George S., Jr. General, *War as I Knew It*. (Houghton Mifflin Company). 1947.

Snyder, Thomas S., and Betty A. Boyce, *Air Force Communications Command: 1938-1991, an Illustrated History*. (Air Force Communications Command Office of History). 1991.

Westenhoff, Charles M., Lt Col, USAF. Military Air Power, the CADRE Digest of Air Power, Opinions and Thoughts. (Air University Press). 1990.

Research Reports

Djuric, Teresa A. H., Lt Col, USAF. <u>Future Command and Control of Aerospace Operations</u>. Carlisle Barracks, PA, 2001. (US Army War College). US Army War College Strategy Research Project.

Hallion, Richard P., Ph.D., SES, USAF. <u>Control of the Air: The Enduring Requirement</u>. Bolling AFB, Washington DC. Air Force History and Museums Program. September, 1999.

Headquarters United States Air Force, Office of Air Force Lessons Learned, AF/XOL. <u>Operation ANACONDA: An Air Power Perspective</u>. February 7, 2005.

Headquarters United States Air Force, Office of Air Force Lessons Learned, AF/A9L. <u>Air Force Support to Hurricane Katrina/Rita Relief Operations</u>. Undated.

Office of the President of the United States, <u>The Federal Response to Hurricane Katrina, Lessons Learned</u>. February, 2006.

Chief of Staff of the Air Force (CSAF) Reading List

CSAF's professional reading list, with links to book reviews, is available on the Air Force web site at: http://www.af.mil/library/csafreading/index.asp. The list is subject to revision. Readers are encouraged to check the website for the most current information.

APPENDIX A

TRANSFER OF FORCES AND COMMAND AUTHORITY

Transfer of Forces

Forces, not command relationships, are transferred between commands. Combatant command (COCOM—command authority) is vested only in commanders of combatant commands or as directed by the President and is nontransferable. Operational control (OPCON) is command authority that may be exercised by commanders at any echelon at or below the level of combatant command and may be delegated within the command. Tactical control (TACON) is the detailed direction and control of movements or maneuvers within the operational area necessary to accomplish assigned missions or tasks.

When the transfer of forces to a joint force will be *permanent* (or for an unknown but long period of time) *forces should be reassigned.* When transfer of forces to a joint force is *temporary*, the forces are *attached* to the gaining command and JFCs will exercise OPCON or TACON, as appropriate, over the attached forces.

Command Authority

COCOM is the command authority over assigned forces vested only in the commanders of combatant commands by title 10, U.S.C., section 164, or as directed by the President in the Unified Command Plan, and cannot be delegated or transferred. COCOM is the authority of a combatant commander to perform those functions of command over assigned forces involving organizing and employing commands and forces, assigning tasks, designating objectives, and giving authoritative direction over all aspects of military operations, joint training (or, in the case of USSOCOM, training of assigned forces), and logistics necessary to accomplish the missions assigned to the command.

OPCON is inherent in COCOM and is the authority to perform those functions of command over subordinate forces involving organizing and employing commands and forces, assigning tasks, designating objectives, and giving authoritative direction necessary to accomplish the mission. OPCON includes authoritative direction over all aspects of military operations and joint training necessary to accomplish missions assigned to the command.

TACON is the command authority over assigned or attached forces or commands or military capability made available for tasking that is limited to the detailed direction and control of movements or maneuvers within the operational area necessary to accomplish assigned missions or tasks. TACON is inherent in OPCON and may be delegated to and exercised by commanders at any echelon at or below the level of combatant command.

Support is a command authority. A support relationship is established by a superior commander between subordinate commanders when one organization should aid, protect, complement, or sustain another force. Support may be exercised by commanders at any echelon at or below the level of combatant command. Several categories of support have been defined for use within a combatant command as appropriate to better characterize the support that should be given. *Support relationships may be categorized as general, mutual, direct, and close.*

Administrative control (ADCON) is the direction or exercise of authority over subordinate or other organizations with respect to administration and support including organization of Service forces, control of resources and equipment, personnel management, unit logistics, individual and unit training, readiness, mobilization, demobilization, discipline, and other matters not included in the operational missions of the subordinate or other organizations. *This is the authority necessary to fulfill military department statutory responsibilities for administration and support.*

Coordinating authority is the authority delegated to a commander or individual for coordinating specific functions and activities involving forces of two or more military departments, two or more joint force components, or two or more forces of the same Service. The commander or individual has the authority to require consultation between the agencies involved, but does not have the authority to compel agreement.

Direct liaison authorized (DIRLAUTH) is that authority granted by a commander (at any level) to a subordinate to directly consult or coordinate an action with a command or agency within or outside of the granting command.

Training and readiness oversight is the authority that combatant commanders may exercise over Reserve forces.

GLOSSARY

Abbreviations and Acronyms

1AF(AFNORTH)	First Air Force (Air Forces Northern)
14AF AFSTRAT-SP	Fourteenth Air Force, Air Force Strategic Command (Space)
8AF/CC	Eighth Air Force Commander
AADC	area air defense commander
ACC	Air Combat Command
ACE	airborne command element
ACCE	air component coordination element
ACS	agile combat support
ADA	air defense artillery
ADCON	administrative control
ADS	air defense sector
AEF	air and space expeditionary force
AETACS	airborne elements of the theater air control system
AETF	air and space expeditionary task force
AEW	air expeditionary wing
AFB	Air Force base
AFDD	Air Force doctrine document
AFFOR	Air Force forces
AFIOC	Air Force Information Operations Center
AFLE	Air Force liaison element
AFNETOPS	Air Force network operations
AFNORTH	Air Force Forces, United States Northern Command
AFOG	Air Force operations group
AFOTTP	Air Force operational tactics, techniques, and procedures
AFRC	Air Force Reserve Command
AFSOC	Air Force Special Operations Command
AFSOD	Air Force special operations detachment
AFSOE	Air Force special operations element

AFSOF	Air Forces special operations forces
AFSPC	Air Force Space Command
AFSWC	Air Force Service Watch Cell
AFTTP(I)	Air Force tactics, techniques, and procedures (interservice)
AIA	Air Intelligence Agency
ALO	air liasion officer
AMC	Air Mobility Command
ANG	Air National Guard
AOB	advanced operating base
AOC	air and space operations center
AOR	area of responsibility
ARC	air Reserve Components
ASOC	air support operations center
ATO	air tasking order
AWACS	airborne warning and control system
BCD	battlefield coordination detachment
BII	base information infrastructure
BOS-I	base operations support-integration
C2	command and control
CAOC	combined air and space operations center
CAP	Civil Air Patrol, crisis action planning
CAT	crisis action team
CC	commander
CDRAFNORTH	Commander, Air Force Forces United States Northern Command
CDRUSEUCOM	Commander, United States European Command
CDRUSNORTHCOM	Commander, United States Northern Command
CDRUSPACOM	Commander, United States Pacific Command
CDRUSSTRATCOM	Commander, United States Strategic Command
CDRUSTRANSCOM	Commander, United States Transportation Command

CFACC	combined force air and space component commander
CJCS	Chairman of the Joint Chiefs of Staff
CJCSI	Chairman of the Joint Chiefs of Staff instruction
CJTF	commander, joint task force
COA	course of action
COCOM	combatant command (command authority)
COE	common operating environment
COMAFFOR	commander, Air Force forces
COMSEC	communications security
CONOPS	concept of operations
CONPLAN	concept plan, or operation plan in concept format
CONR	continental United States North American Aerospace Defense Command Region
CONUS	continental United States
COP	common operational picture
CP	command post
CRC	control and reporting center
CSAF	Chief of Staff, United States Air Force
CSC2	combat support command and control
CSS	communications systems support
DCA	defensive counterair
DIA	Defense Intelligence Agency
DII	defense information infrastructure
DIRMOBFOR-AIR	director of mobility forces-Air
DIRLAUTH	direct liasion authorized
DIRSPACEFOR	director of space forces
DISA	Defense Information Systems Agency
DISN	Defense Information Systems Network
DITSCAP	Department of Defense information technology security certification and accreditation process
DOD	Department of Defense
DODD	Department of Defense directive

DRU	direct reporting unit
DSCA	defense support of civil authorities
EAP	emergency actions procedures
EBAO	effects-based approach to operations
EMTF	expeditionary mobility task force
EOC	emergency operations center
EP	emergency preparedness
EW	electronic warfare
FAC (A)	forward air controller (airborne)
FOA	field operating agency
FOB	forward operating base
GCC	geographic combatant commander
GCCS	global command and control system
GIG	global information grid
GNO	global network operations
GPS	global positioning system
GTACS	ground theater air control system
HD	homeland defense
HS	homeland security
IA	information assurance
ICC	installation control center
IM	information management
IMP	information management plan
IO	information operations; international organization
IQT	initial qualification training
ISR	intelligence, surveillance, and reconnaissance
IT	information technology

JAEP	joint air and space estimate process
JAOC	joint air and space operations center
JAOP	joint air and space operations plan
JARN	joint air request net
JCS	Joint Chiefs of Staff
JDN	joint data network
JFACC	joint force air and space component commander
JFC	joint force commander
JFCC Space	Joint Functional Component Command Space
JOA	joint operations area
JOC	joint operations center
JOPES	joint operation planning and execution system
JOPP	joint operation planning process
JP	joint publication
JSOACC	joint special operations air component commander
JSOTF	joint special operations task force
JSpOC	Joint Space Operations Center
JSTARS	joint surveillance target attack radar system
JTA	joint technical architecture
JTAC	joint terminal attack controller
JTF	joint task force
LNO	liaison officer
MAJCOM	major command
MAPE	monitor, assess, plan, and execute (model)
MARLO	Marine liaison officer
MOA	memorandum of agreement
MOU	memorandum of understanding
MQT	mission qualification training

NAF	numbered Air Force
NALE	naval and amphibious liaison element
NATO	North Atlantic Treaty Organization
NCO	network-centric operations
NCW	network-centric warfare
NetA	network attack
NetD	network defense
NETOPS	network operations
NGO	non-governmental organization
NIPRNET	non-secure internet protocol router network
NMCC	National Military Command Center
NMCS	National Military Command System
NORAD	North American Aerospace Defense Command
NSA	National Security Agency
NW Ops	network warfare operations
OODA Loop	observe, orient, decide and act (loop)
OPCON	operational control
OPLAN	operation plan
OPORD	operations order
PACAF	Pacific Air Forces
RAMCC	regional air movement control center
ROE	rules of engagement
SAA	senior airfield authority
SADL	situation awareness data link
SECAF	Secretary of the Air Force
SecDef	Secretary of Defense
SIPRNET	secret internet protocol router network
SO	special operations

SOCCE	special operations command and control element
SODO	senior offensive duty officer
SOF	special operations forces
SOLE	special operations liaison element
SSAA	systems security authorization agreements
STO	space tasking order
TACC	tanker airlift control center
TACON	tactical control
TACP	tactical air control party
TACS	theater air control system
TADL	tactical digital information link
TADIL	tactical digital information link
TAGS	theater air-ground system
TPFDD	time-phased force and deployment data
TSOC	theater special operations command
UCMJ	Uniform Code of Military Justice
UCP	Unified Command Plan
UNAAF	Unified Action Armed Forces
USAF	United States Air Force
USAFE	United States Air Forces Europe
U.S.C.	United States Code
USEUCOM	United States European Command
USJFCOM	United States Joint Forces Command
USNORTHCOM	United States Northern Command
USSOCOM	United States Special Operations Command
USSTRATCOM	United States Strategic Command
USTRANSCOM	United States Transportation Command
WMP	war and mobilization plan

Definitions

administrative control. Direction or exercise of authority over subordinate or other organizations in respect to administration and support, including organization of Service forces, control of resources and equipment, personnel management, unit logistics, individual and unit training, readiness, mobilization, demobilization, discipline, and other matters not included in the operational missions of the subordinate or other organizations. Also called **ADCON.** (JP 1-02)

air force network operations. The operation and defense of the communications system supporting the Air Force's provisioned portion of the Global Information Grid. Also called AFNETOPS. (AFDD 2-8)

apportionment. In the general sense, distribution for planning of limited resources among competing requirements. Specific apportionments (e.g., air sorties and forces for planning) are described as apportionment of air sorties and forces for planning, etc. (JP 1-02)

apportionment (air). The determination and assignment of the total expected effort by percentage and/or by priority that should be devoted to the various air operations for a given period of time. Also called **air apportionment**. See also **apportionment.** (JP 1-02)

assign. 1. To place units or personnel in an organization where such placement is relatively permanent, and/or where such organization controls and administers the units or personnel for the primary function, or greater portion of the functions, of the unit or personnel. 2. To detail individuals to specific duties or functions where such duties or functions are primary and/or relatively permanent. See also **attach**. (JP 1-02)

attach. 1. The placement of units or personnel in an organization where such placement is relatively temporary. 2. The detailing of individuals to specific functions where such functions are secondary or relatively temporary, e.g., attached for quarters and rations; attached for flying duty. See also **assign**. (JP 1-02)

combatant command (command authority). Nontransferable command authority established by title 10, ("Armed Forces"), United States Code, section 164, exercised only by commanders of unified or specified combatant commands unless otherwise directed by the President or the SecDef. Combatant command (command authority) cannot be delegated and is the authority of a combatant commander to perform those functions of command over assigned forces involving organizing and employing commands and forces, assigning tasks, designating objectives, and giving authoritative direction over all aspects of military operations, joint training, and logistics necessary to accomplish the missions assigned to the command. Combatant command (command authority) should be exercised through the commanders of subordinate organizations. Normally, this authority is exercised through subordinate joint force commanders and Service and/or functional component commanders. Combatant command (command authority) provides full authority to organize and employ commands and forces as the combatant commander considers necessary to accomplish assigned missions. Operational control is inherent in combatant command (command authority). Also called **COCOM**. (JP 1-02)

command. The authority that a commander in the Armed Forces lawfully exercises over subordinates by virtue of rank or assignment. Command includes the authority and responsibility for effectively using available resources and for planning the employment of, organizing, directing, coordinating, and controlling military forces for the accomplishment of assigned missions. It also includes responsibility for health, welfare, morale, and discipline of assigned personnel. (JP 1-02)

command and control. The exercise of authority and direction by a properly designated commander over assigned and attached forces in the accomplishment of the mission. Command and control functions are performed through an arrangement of personnel, equipment, communications, facilities, and procedures employed by a commander in planning, directing, coordinating, and controlling forces and operations in the accomplishment of the mission. Also called **C2**. (JP 1-02)

defense information infrastructure. The shared or interconnected system of computers, communications, data applications, security, people, training, and other support structures serving DOD local, national, and worldwide information needs. The defense information infrastructure connects DOD mission support, command and control, and intelligence computers through voice, telecommunications, imagery, video, and multimedia services. It provides information processing and services to subscribers over the defense information systems network and includes command and control, tactical, intelligence, and commercial communications systems used to transmit DOD information. Also called **DII**. (JP 1-02)

distributed operations. The process of conducting operations from independent or interdependent nodes in a teaming manner. Some operational planning or decision-making may occur from outside the joint area of operations. The goal of a distributed operation is to support the operational commander in the field; it is not a method of command from the rear. See also split operations. (AFDD 2-8)

effects-based approach to operations. Operations that are planned, executed, assessed and adapted to influence or change system behavior or capabilities in order to achieve desired outcomes. Also called **EBAO**. (Note:

Sometimes colloquially but incorrectly referred to as "effects-based operations," or EBO) (AFDD 2)

force protection. Actions taken to prevent or mitigate hostile actions against Department of Defense personnel (to include family members), resources, facilities, and critical information. These actions conserve the force's fighting potential so it can be applied at the decisive time and place and incorporate the coordinated and synchronized offensive and defensive measures to enable the effective employment of the joint force while degrading opportunities for the enemy. Force protection does not include actions to defeat the enemy or protect against accidents, weather, or disease. Also called **FP**. (JP 1-02) [*An integrated application of offensive and defensive actions that deter, detect, preempt, mitigate, or negate threats against or hazards to Air Force air and space operations and assets, based on an acceptable level of risk.*] (AFDD 2-4.1) {Italicized definition in brackets applies only to the Air Force and is offered for clarity.}

information. 1. Facts, data, or instructions in any medium or form. 2. The meaning that a human assigns to data by means of the known conventions used in their representation. (JP 1-02)

information operations. Actions taken to affect adversary information and information systems while defending one's own information and information systems. Also called **IO**. (JP 1-02) [*Information operations are the integrated employment of the core capabilities of influence operations, electronic warfare operations, network warfare operations, in concert with specified integrated control enablers, to influence, disrupt, corrupt or usurp adversarial human and automated decision making while protecting our own.*] (AFDD 2-5) {Italicized definition in brackets applies only to the Air Force and is offered for clarity.}

intelligence. 1. The product resulting from the collection, processing, integration, analysis, evaluation, and interpretation of available information concerning foreign countries or areas. 2. Information and knowledge about an adversary obtained through observation, investigation, analysis, or understanding. (JP 1-02)

joint force. A general term applied to a force composed of significant elements, assigned or attached, of two or more Military Departments, operating under a single joint force commander. See also **joint force commander**. (JP 1-02)

joint force air component commander. The commander within a unified command, subordinate unified command, or joint task force responsible to the establishing commander for making recommendations on the proper employment of assigned, attached, and/or made available for tasking air forces; planning and coordinating air operations; or accomplishing such operational missions as may be assigned. The joint force air component commander is given the authority necessary to accomplish missions and tasks assigned by the establishing commander. Also called **JFACC**. (JP 1-02) [*The joint force air and space component commander (JFACC) uses the joint air and space operations center to command and control the integrated air and space effort to meet the joint force commander's objectives. This title emphasizes the Air Force position that air power and space power together create effects that cannot be achieved through air or space power alone.*] [AFDD 2] {Italicized words in brackets apply only to the Air Force and are offered for clarity.}

joint force commander. A general term applied to a combatant commander, subunified commander, or joint task force commander authorized to exercise combatant command (command authority) or operational control over a joint force. Also called **JFC**. See also **joint force**. (JP 1-02)

joint task force. A joint force that is constituted and so designated by the Secretary of Defense, a combatant commander, a subunified commander, or an existing joint task force commander. Also called **JTF**. (JP 1-02)

military strategy. The art and science of employing the armed forces of a nation to secure the objectives of national policy by the application of force or the threat of force. (JP 1-02)

national strategy. The art and science of developing and using the political, economic, and psychological powers of a nation, together with its armed forces, during peace and war, to secure national objectives. (JP 1-02)

network attack. The employment of network-based capabilities to destroy, disrupt, corrupt, or usurp information resident in or transiting through networks. Networks include telephony and data services networks. Also called **NetA**. (AFDD 2-5)

network operations. The integrated planning and employment of military capabilities to provide the friendly net environment needed to plan, control and execute military operations and conduct Service functions. NETOPS provides operational planning and control. It involves time-critical, operational-level decisions that direct configuration changes and information routing. NETOPS risk management and command and control decisions are based on a fused assessment of intelligence, ongoing operations, commander's intent, blue and gray situation, net health, and net security. NETOPS provides the three operational elements of information assurance, network/system management, and information dissemination management. Also called **NETOPS**. (AFDD 2-5)

network warfare operations. Network warfare operations are the integrated planning and employment of military capabilities to achieve desired effects across the interconnected analog and digital portion of the battlespace. Network warfare operations are conducted in the information domain through the dynamic combination of hardware, software, data, and human interaction. Also called **NW Ops**. (AFDD 2-5)

operational control. Transferable command authority that may be exercised by commanders at any echelon at or below the level of combatant command. Operational control is inherent in combatant command (command authority). Operational control may be delegated and is the authority to perform those functions of command over subordinate forces involving organizing and employing commands and forces, assigning tasks, designating objectives, and giving authoritative direction necessary to accomplish the mission. Operational control includes authoritative direction over all aspects of military operations and joint training necessary to accomplish missions assigned to the command. Operational control should be exercised through the commanders of subordinate organizations. Normally this authority is exercised through subordinate joint force commanders and Service and/or functional component commanders. Operational control normally provides full authority to organize commands and forces and to employ those forces as the commander in operational control considers necessary to accomplish assigned missions. Operational control does not, in and of itself, include authoritative direction for logistics or matters of administration, discipline, internal organization, or unit training. Also called **OPCON**. (JP 1-02)

operational environment. A composite of the conditions, circumstances, and influences that affect the employment of military forces and bear on the decisions of the unit commander. (JP 1-02)

operational level of war. The level of war at which campaigns and major operations are planned, conducted, and sustained to accomplish strategic objectives within theaters or areas of operations. Activities at this level link tactics and strategy by establishing operational objectives needed to accomplish the strategic objectives, sequencing events to achieve the operational objectives, initiating actions, and applying resources to bring about and sustain these events. These activities imply a broader dimension of time or space than do tactics; they ensure the logistic and administrative support of tactical forces, and provide the means by which tactical successes are exploited to achieve strategic objectives. (JP 1-02)

operational risk management. The systematic process of identifying hazards, assessing risks, analyzing risk control measures, making control decisions, implementing risk controls, and supervising and reviewing the process. Commanders accept the residual risks. (AFI 91-213)

reachback. The process of obtaining products, services, and applications, or forces, equipment, or materiel from Air Force organizations that are not forward deployed. (AFDD 2)

reconnaissance. A mission undertaken to obtain, by visual observation or other detection methods, information about the activities and resources of an enemy or potential enemy, or to secure data concerning the meteorological, hydrographic, or geographic characteristics of a particular area. (JP 1-02)

senior airfield authority. The senior airfield authority is an individual designated by the joint force commander to be responsible for the control, operation, and maintenance of an airfield to include runways, associated taxiways, parking ramps, land, and facilities whose proximity affect airfield operations. Also called **SAA**. (JP 3-17)

special operations. Operations conducted by specially organized, trained, and equipped military and paramilitary forces to achieve military, political, economic, or informational objectives by unconventional military means in hostile, denied, or politically sensitive areas. These operations are conducted across the full range of military operations, independently or in coordination with operations of conventional, non-special operations forces. Political-military considerations frequently shape special operations, requiring clandestine, covert, or low visibility techniques and oversight at the national level. Special operations differ from conventional operations in degree of physical and political risk, operational techniques, mode of employment, independence from friendly support, and dependence on detailed operational intelligence and indigenous assets. Also called **SO**. (JP 1-02)

spectrum management. Planning, coordinating, and managing joint use of the electromagnetic spectrum through operational, engineering, and administrative procedures, with the objective of enabling electronics systems to perform their functions in the intended environment without causing or suffering unacceptable interference. (AFI 33-118)

split operations. One type of distributed operations. It describes those distributed operations conducted by a single command and control (C2) entity that is separated between two or more geographic locations. A single commander must have oversight of all aspects of a split C2 operation. (AFDD 2-8)

strategic level of war. The level of war at which a nation, often as a member of a group of nations, determines national or multinational (alliance or coalition) security objectives and guidance, and develops and uses national resources to accomplish those objectives. Activities at this level establish national and multinational military objectives; sequence initiatives; define limits and assess risks for the use of military and other instruments of national power; develop global plans or theater war plans to achieve these objectives; and provide military forces and other capabilities in accordance with strategic plans. (JP 1-02)

strategy. The art and science of developing and using political, economic, psychological, and military forces as necessary during peace and war, to afford the maximum support to policies, in order to increase the probabilities and favorable consequences of victory and to lessen the chances of defeat. (JP 1-02)

surveillance. The systematic observation of aerospace, surface or subsurface areas, places, persons, or things, by visual, aural, electronic, photographic, or other means. (JP 1-02)

tactical control. Command authority over assigned or attached forces or commands, or military capability or forces made available for tasking, that is limited to the detailed and, usually, local direction and control of movements or maneuvers necessary to accomplish missions or tasks assigned. Tactical control is inherent in operational control. Tactical control may be delegated to, and exercised at any level at or below the level of combatant command. Also called **TACON.** (JP 1-02)

tactical level of war. The level of war at which battles and engagements are planned and executed to accomplish military objectives assigned to tactical units or task forces. Activities at this level focus on the ordered arrangement and maneuver of combat elements in relation to each other and to the enemy to achieve combat objectives. (JP 1-02)

tactics. 1. The employment of units in combat. 2. The ordered arrangement and maneuver of units in relation to each other and/or to the enemy in order to use their full potentialities. (JP 1-02)

theater. The geographical area outside the continental United States for which a commander of a combatant command has been assigned responsibility. (JP 1-02)

war. Open and often prolonged conflict between nations (or organized groups within nations) to achieve national objectives. (AFDD 1)

www.ingramcontent.com/pod-product-compliance
Lightning Source LLC
Chambersburg PA
CBHW080300290526
45790CB00005B/1881